PLANET FRIENDLY
BAKING

SUSTAINABLE RECIPES FOR EVERY SEASON

HONEYWELL
BAKES

First edition printed in 2024 in the UK
ISBN: 978-1-915538-31-4

Written by: Rebecca Honeywell-Ward
& Laura Slack

Edited by: Emily Readman

Photography by: Rebecca Honeywell-Ward,
Kayley Miles, Laura Slack & Stu Cooper

Designed by: Paul Cocker

Sales: Emma Toogood

Contributors: Cara Snowden, Ben Doyle
& Sophia Derby

Printed in the UK by: Bell & Bain Ltd

Published by Meze Publishing Limited
Unit 1b, 2 Kelham Square
Kelham Riverside
Sheffield S3 8SD
Web: www.mezepublishing.co.uk
Telephone: 0114 275 7709
Email: info@mezepublishing.co.uk

Honeywell Bakes Ltd
www.honeywellbakes.com
hellohoney@honeywellbakes.com

TO MUM,
THE ORIGINAL PLANET FRIENDLY BAKER
AND THE QUEEN OF SUBSTITUTIONS.

CONTENTS

INTRODUCTION

"NEVER DOUBT THAT A SMALL GROUP OF THOUGHTFUL, COMMITTED CITIZENS CAN CHANGE THE WORLD. INDEED, IT'S THE ONLY THING THAT EVER HAS."

– MARGARET MEAD

This book brings together delicious, creative recipes from Honeywell Bakes and my friends and family, as well a passion for taking care of our wonderful planet and all that lives on it.

When I was young, I'd come running into the house straight from school looking for one thing: cake. Mum is firmly against processed food, and shop-bought cake was rarely allowed in the house. She did, however, believe that growing, active children should have a slice of homemade cake after school. It probably gave her 15 minutes of peace before the evening of chaos began. My childhood memories are therefore filled with the smells of baking. Squidgy chocolate cake, sticky flapjack, and tins of dulce de leche eaten with a spoon (which was used as a bribe to get us all walking up hills at the weekends). Mum's fervent belief in cake as an essential part of any given day has certainly been passed down to me.

I am the oldest of seven siblings and we were brought up in a busy, noisy household. Despite the chaos and never-ending washing, our childhood was filled with sustainable choices made by our parents that were quite unusual for that time: reusable nappies, fruit and veg from the local greengrocer (and never ever in plastic), and clothing purchases carefully considered and handed down from child to child (there was a definite benefit to being the oldest there!). We knew what our food was and where it came from, whether that was the veg grown in the garden or the eggs laid by the hens outside.

Growing up in the Northamptonshire countryside, we were surrounded by nature. We didn't have a TV, instead spending our time at the farm next door, or in the fields searching the hedgerows for birds' nests, inspecting insects in puddles, or stomping through snow, red-faced and pulling a sledge behind us, our feet encased in plastic bags beneath our wellies to stave off the cold. Nature was everywhere, and we took it for granted. We ate wild, juicy blackberries until our stomachs hurt, we delighted in finding teeny tiny strawberries that would burst with flavour, and we would suck the sweet, honeyed nectar from nettle flowers.

When I first learnt to drive, the small windscreen of my ancient Beetle would be covered with insects after every trip. I spent hours polishing them off the round, wide eyed headlights, trying to make the chrome sparkle, only for them to be splattered all over it once more on the next drive to visit a friend.

Where are those insects now? Nowadays, there are a lot less insects and the chances of getting a mouthful of flies is much lower. This is not as good as it sounds. Those insects are a vital part of life on Earth; they are needed for pollination, to feed the birds, and are part of our overall ecosystem. By doing things slightly differently, we can help the insects, birds and wildlife thrive, whilst still enjoying beautiful, tasty treats.

Honeywell Bakes grew from the kitchen table with a love of people and the planet at the heart of all our decisions from the very beginning. Along the way, we have learnt many things, which we share with you here in an easily digestible and hopefully inspiring way. You will find information about utensils, reducing food waste (did you know sour milk makes the most incredible fluffy pancakes?), regenerative farming, and more.

Together, we can create a balanced world in which people and the planet thrive. Let us eat cake!

Rebecca – Honeywell Bakes' Founder

ABOUT HONEYWELL BAKES

Honeywell Bakes began in 2012 with a vision of bringing creative baking to everyone. We started with the idea of posting out all manner of delicious, beautiful bakes, but quickly settled on hand-iced biscuits as our main focus. Biscuits are so adaptable and can be any shape, and when iced beautifully by our wonderful biscuit artists, they make a wonderful gift. They also have a naturally long shelf life and are easy to post without breaking.

The planet has always been at the heart of what we do; we've always used locally produced ingredients where possible and packaging that is compostable or recyclable. Within a few years, we moved from a home kitchen to a dedicated premises in a converted barn in the Northamptonshire countryside, and as we've grown, so has our team. We now employ 18 local women, who are all amazing, and I no longer have to bake and ice every order myself!

We added artisan baking kits and monthly baking subscriptions to our repertoire in 2018, which include pre-weighed ingredients to make baking at home easy and fun. The subscriptions are designed to teach and inspire children and adults alike; whether you're a beginner or a seasoned baker, the kits will offer you something new.

Honeywell Bakes has been a certified B Corp since June 2022, and it's an achievement we are extremely proud of – it's not easy to become certified! B Corporations are businesses that meet the highest standards of verified social and environmental performance, public transparency, and legal accountability to balance profit and purpose. What this means in practical terms is that we try our hardest to do more good than harm.

As part of our commitment, we donate to 1% For The Planet with every sale, meaning we are committed to giving back to nature.

10 QUICK STEPS TO MAKE BAKING MORE SUSTAINABLE

1. Choose organic and/or regeneratively produced flour. It will have far less chemicals, which is better for the planet (soil, water and wildlife) and for our health.

2. Use local, seasonal ingredients where you can.

3. Choose free-range eggs. The hens are healthier and won't need as much food, which is often imported from abroad, as they will forage for themselves.

4. Choose a plant-based butter block or use organic British butter.

5. Buy food with less packaging, for example from a refill shop or greengrocer.

6. Check the labels of the products you buy and make sure any palm oil is RSPO certified. Non-RSPO palm oil is very problematic from both an environmental and social perspective. Palm oil can be a sustainable product when produced sensitively, and alternatives can be more damaging to the planet.

7. Reuse almost everything! Think before throwing anything out: tin foil, cling film, baking parchment, and takeaway tubs can be washed and reused many times.

8. Buy silicone baking sheets (also called reusable non-stick baking liners) and cut them to the size of your most used pans so you don't need to use baking parchment or greaseproof paper. There's often no need for lining cake tins – just grease and dust thoroughly with flour or cocoa powder and they will turn out perfectly well.

9. Use non-toxic washing up liquid, surface cleaner, dishwasher tablets and cloths. Nancy Birtwhistle is the Clean Green Queen, so look her up if you need inspiration.

10. Only buy what you need and compost any food that really can't be used.

NOTES ON INGREDIENTS

"ORGANIC FARMING IS BETTER FOR PEOPLE, THE PLANET, WILDLIFE AND ANIMALS."

– THE SOIL ASSOCIATION

We always choose organic ingredients where we can, but this can make for an expensive shop! If you only do one thing, making some swaps to organic ingredients will make a great difference to the planet.

FLOUR
Choose organic and/or regeneratively farmed flour where you can.

BUTTER
We use organic, salted butter or a plant-based butter block in all our recipes. Plant-based butter blocks are a sustainable choice with a lower carbon footprint than standard butter. Plant-based unsweetened milk can also be used in place of cow's milk.

SUGAR
Sugar is a complex ingredient as it requires a lot of chemical input to grow in the UK, meaning it needs to be shipped from warmer climates if it is grown more naturally. It's better to buy organic and/or fairtrade where possible.

EGGS
Always free-range medium eggs, and organic if possible. There's no real need for large or extra large eggs, and there's evidence that these can be harmful for the chickens. Eggs have a lower carbon footprint than dairy, but it's best to use them mindfully and ensure that they are not wasted.

For plant-based bakes, eggs in cookies and brownies can be replaced with 1 teaspoon of baking soda combined with 1 tablespoon of vinegar. It can be harder to replace eggs in cakes, but we have included some plant-based recipes. Aquafaba is a good egg replacement in yeasted bread recipes and meringues. Oggs also make excellent egg replacement products and have an online 'How To' guide.

VANILLA
Real vanilla extract tastes better and is better for the planet. Where vanilla is planted, biodiversity is increased, so it's always better to choose real vanilla rather than the chemically created vanilla that is often called vanilla essence.

WHAT SHOULD WE DO ABOUT PALM OIL?
Palm oil is a major contributor to the deforestation of some of the world's most biodiverse forests, but it is an incredibly efficient crop and produces more oil per land area than any other equivalent vegetable oil crop. To get the same amount of alternative oils, like soybean, coconut, or sunflower oil, you would need between four and ten times more land. Therefore, according to WWF, the best thing we can do is support sustainable palm oil and avoid boycotts, since we know substituting other vegetable oils can lead to even further environmental and social harm. Look for the RSPO logo to check if the palm oil is sustainable; it's also possible to look up companies online and find out where they source their palm oil.

A NOTE ON OVEN TEMPERATURES
We've included the temperature for fan assisted ovens, so please add 20°C for conventional ovens. Know your oven and only turn it on 5 to 10 minutes before you need it, unless it's very slow to preheat. This will save energy (and money!).

PLANT-BASED RECIPES
The following recipes are plant-based bakes, when using plant-based butter and milk: Dan's Fruit Crumble (page 44), Mum's Scones (page 30), Mum's Flapjack (page 32), Mum's Raspberry Jam (page 110), Raspberry Croissant (page 72), Laura's Fruit Shortbread (page 106), Jill's Ginger Biscuits (page 92), Grandma Honey's 'Grassmere Gingerbread' (page 146), Apple and Date Hand Pies (page 132), Apple Scrap Jelly (page 158), Clare's Mincemeat (page 180), Mince Pies with Frangipane Topping (page 182), Emily's Boozy Coffee Cupcakes (page 170).

KEY UTENSILS: BAKING EQUIPMENT

"PURCHASING SECOND HAND PUTS THOSE THINGS BACK INTO CIRCULATION, REDUCING THEIR OVERALL ENVIRONMENTAL FOOTPRINT"

– THE CENTER FOR BIOLOGICAL DIVERSITY

USE WHAT YOU HAVE, BUY SECOND HAND

Whilst we would always encourage people to use what they have, there are some items that you may need to add to your collection. Before buying anything, have a good rummage in the back of your cabinets in case there is anything lurking there, and if you can borrow items or buy second hand that's better than getting new.

THESE RECIPES ARE ADAPTABLE

The list overleaf includes items that will be very useful for a fairly frequent baker, but do be creative and don't worry if you don't have it all. There are some recipes that call for more unusual tins, such as a bundt tin, but most recipes are adaptable (and this cake will also bake perfectly well in a normal round tin).

If a recipe calls for a square tin, you can use a round one, or if it calls for a 7-inch tin, a 6-inch or 8-inch tin would also work; the bake will just be shallower or deeper! Just be aware that a thicker cake will generally take longer to cook, so keep an eye on your bakes and adjust cooking times according to adaptions you make.

CHOOSE HIGH QUALITY UTENSILS

In general, it's better to buy the best quality you can afford. For example, there are some lovely stainless steel pans and enamel cake tins available which contain no chemicals and last a lifetime, even becoming heirloom items that can be passed on for generations to come, and so won't end up in landfill.

CHEMICALS

Some cookware can contain chemicals that make their way into food and into the water system when washed. Try to choose stainless steel, cast iron, enamel, ceramic or glass, as these won't contain PFAS chemicals.

CARING FOR YOUR BAKING EQUIPMENT

Follow the washing and care instructions! This will mean your items last, helping you create beautiful bakes for years to come.

USEFUL EQUIPMENT

Scales – Digital or analogue, but digital are more precise. Rechargeable versions are available. If you don't have scales, you can use cup measurement equivalents which you can find online by searching for conversions, however they are not very accurate.

Heavy-bottomed stainless steel saucepans – The heavy bottom stops things burning and stainless steel is very strong, so it lasts a long time.

Wooden spoon – Hand wash, dry well, and these will last indefinitely.

Spatula – Very useful, but if you don't have one, you'll manage!

Measuring jug – We prefer glass as they can be microwaved. You can weigh liquids if you don't have one.

Silicone sheets or compostable baking parchment – Don't forget, you can simply use a little flour and butter for your cakes!

Skewer – For testing cakes. A fine metal skewer is best, but a cocktail stick will work too!

NICE TO HAVE

These items are helpful, and whilst not necessary, if you are a frequent baker they are worth investing in.

Reusable piping bags – We find that silicone versions work best and are really easy to wash.

Piping tips – The most useful are a star tip and tips with 2mm and 5mm holes

Silicone baking sheets – These can be cut to size to line the bottom of rectangular, square and circular baking tins, meaning you no longer need to buy and discard baking parchment. They last years.

Cookie cutters – A set of circles fluted on one side and straight on the other are very versatile, and you can pick up fun shapes in cooking shops if you fancy being creative. Always hand wash and dry thoroughly and they will last forever.

Stand mixer – Very useful if you regularly make bread. Out of all the ones we've used, KitchenAids last extremely well, can be serviced, and have replaceable parts.

Cake tins – Ideally we'd have:
- Two shallow, circular tins
- Rectangular baking tray
- Springform or pie tin
- Loaf tin
- Muffin/cupcake tin

Measuring spoons – You can also use the teaspoons and dessert spoons you have, or weigh the ingredients. A teaspoon is approximately 5g and a tablespoon is 15g.

Rolling pin – In a pinch, use a wine bottle!

Sieve – You can do without, but you may need to work harder to get rid of lumps.

Electric whisk – It's worth investing in a good quality one if you can as it will last well.

Wire cooling rack – Choose one with small holes.

Mixing bowls – Various sizes, in glass, metal, or enamel ideally, as plastic can hold grease or odours which can make some things harder to make, e.g. fluffy meringues. Glass can also be microwaved.

TOP TIPS

Read the recipe thoroughly – This will help you understand what is needed and when, which is important with some recipes, such as when ovens need preheating.

Know your oven – How long does it take to heat up? Don't waste energy preheating for too long!

Plan bakes – For example, meringues cook for a long time on a low heat so you can turn your oven off before they are done.

Think of alternatives – If you do not have something that a recipe calls for, see what you can use instead of buying something. No cookie cutter? Use a knife to cut around a jam jar lid. No rolling pin? A wine bottle will do the trick!

Check out recipes for food that is past its prime – Sour milk, stale bread, over-ripe bananas - all of these can be used.

Grow your own – It can be quite easy to grow some fruit. Raspberries and strawberries don't take too much space and fruit trees including apple, pear and plum can be grown espalier-style along fences.

SPRING

The season where everything starts to sprout and things begin to feel very hopeful. It's heartening to see bulbs poking up as the daffodils, tulips, and blossoms spring into life. In the UK, fruit begins to ripen, rhubarb and gooseberries are in season, and towards the end of May, the strawberry season starts. Citrus fruits are in season abroad and therefore are common in our shops; we suggest choosing organic, fairtrade and unwaxed fruit when you can. Checking the labels and picking fruit that comes from closer neighbours, such as France, Italy, Morocco, and Spain, means it won't have travelled as far, so the carbon footprint will be lower.

The idea of picnics starts to form in our minds, and as soon as there's a sunny Saturday, we think of having a barbecue, only to be stuck in the cold – freezing ourselves in true British fashion – until all of the food is eaten. It's still cool enough to enjoy a heartening, warm crumble or spend a day in the kitchen making croissants without feeling like you're missing out on being outside. A brisk walk followed by a steaming hot cup of tea and a freshly baked cake is just what is needed. When Easter arrives, it's a given that we will all eat plenty of chocolate, and it simply wouldn't be Easter without fresh hot cross buns.

As the first flowers bloom, some of the edible ones (roses, violas and pansies) can be picked and pressed to adorn bakes later in the year. Pick them on a dry day and make sure they are chemical-free. Press the petals between heavy books with pieces of parchment either side of the blooms, or use a flower press. If you fancy growing your own fruit and veg, now is the time to start. Planting native varieties will provide food and cover for a range of wildlife, as well as food for you!

SQUIDGY CHOCOLATE CAKE

There is no celebration that this cake isn't perfect for, and it's become a recipe our family is famous for. It's the perfect chocolate cake: moist, but not dense. It is very versatile and is our most used birthday cake recipe; top it with fruit, drizzle it with caramel and pile popcorn on top, or simply ice it and stick a candle in the middle.

Serves: 12
Prep time: 40 minutes
Cooking time: 40 minutes
Oven temp: 160°C fan

FOR THE CAKE

220g butter, softened
340g caster sugar
3 eggs
650ml milk
1 ½ tsp vanilla extract
340g plain flour
65g cocoa powder
½ tsp cream of tartar
2 tsp bicarbonate of soda

FOR THE ICING

340g icing sugar
60g cocoa powder
125g butter, softened
A little hot milk

Prepare two 8-inch cake tins by greasing them with butter then dusting with cocoa – simply add some to the tins and tap and rotate them until the base and sides are covered. Weigh out any excess cocoa to use for the cake.

In a large bowl, cream the butter and sugar using an electric whisk or wooden spoon until pale and fluffy. Add the eggs and milk and mix well – it will look curdled at this stage!

Add the vanilla extract then sift the remaining dry ingredients into the mixture. Mix well until smooth. This is a wetter than average cake mixture, so don't worry if it seems runny.

Divide the cake mixture evenly between the two tins and bake for approximately 40 minutes. When cooked, the cake will spring back if gently pressed, or a fine skewer will come out clean when inserted into the centre of the cake. Once baked, remove from the oven and leave to cool for 10 minutes before removing the cakes from the tins and setting them on a wire rack to cool completely.

For the icing, sift the icing sugar and cocoa into a bowl. Add the butter and mix together – go gently to avoid a cloud in your kitchen! Add hot milk, a little at a time, until you have a thick, spreadable icing.

When the cakes have fully cooled, spread about half of the icing evenly on one cake before placing the second cake on top. Spread the remaining icing on top of the cake and decorate with any fruit or toppings that you have to hand.

BAKER'S TIP

In the unlikely event your cake isn't completely devoured and it goes a little stale, warm up a slice until the icing melts and the cake is soft again, then serve with a scoop of vanilla ice cream. Bliss!

JESSICA'S PANCAKES

Jessica, my daughter, loves these delicious American-style pancakes, and they are even better when made with buttermilk or sour milk. It gives them extra fluffiness and a bit of a tang that works perfectly with the toppings of your choice. They are always served at every child's birthday in our house. Trust us and give them a try!

Makes: 12 pancakes
Prep time: 10 minutes
Cooking time: 30 minutes

FOR THE PANCAKES

200g self-raising flour

1 tsp baking powder

A pinch of salt

1 egg, beaten

300ml buttermilk (or slightly sour milk)

10g butter, melted, plus extra for cooking

FOR THE TOPPING (SUGGESTED)

Mixed berries or compote, warmed

Chocolate spread

Maple syrup

Nuts, chopped

Fresh fruit, sliced

Mix the flour, baking powder and a pinch of salt into a large bowl. Then, add the beaten egg and milk and whisk together to make a smooth, thick batter. Finally, beat in the melted butter.

Melt a little butter in a non-stick frying pan over a medium heat. Drop roughly a large, heaped tablespoon per pancake into the pan. Cook as many as will comfortably fit in the pan, leaving a little room for spreading. If you wish, you can drop some blueberries or slices of banana onto the top of the pancake at this stage. They will sink into the batter as it cooks.

When small bubbles appear on the surface of a pancake, after approximately 2 to 3 minutes, flip it over and cook for a further 2 to 3 minutes until golden.

Serve piled high with a generous helping of the toppings of your choice!

BAKER'S TIP

Make your own buttermilk by adding 1 tablespoon of lemon or lime juice to 300ml of milk and leaving it in a warm place for 10 minutes. This works with soya milk, too.

RASPBERRY AND WHITE CHOCOLATE ECLAIRS

Eclairs make an impressive treat and are not too difficult to bake if the steps are followed carefully. You could fill them with whipped cream and top them with chocolate for a simpler bake or try experimenting with flavour combinations.

Makes: 10-12
Prep time: 45 minutes
Cooking time: 45 minutes
Oven temp: 200°C fan

FOR THE CHOUX PASTRY

60ml milk

50g butter

60ml water

75g plain flour

2 eggs, beaten

FOR THE CREAM FILLING

4 egg yolks

60g caster sugar

2 tsp cornflour

25g plain flour

280ml milk

10g freeze-dried raspberries, or 60g fresh raspberries

FOR THE TOPPING

Raspberry juice (reserved from filling)

100g icing sugar

20g white chocolate

1 tbsp freeze-dried or fresh raspberries

YOU WILL NEED

Piping bag with a 2cm tip

To make the choux pastry, combine the milk, butter and water in a saucepan and gently melt the butter but don't allow the liquid to bubble. Once the butter has completely melted, bring to a fast boil. Immediately turn off the heat, tip in the flour, and beat vigorously with a wooden spoon until you have a smooth dough that comes away from the pan's edges. Cool for 10 minutes before gradually adding the beaten egg and mixing until the dough reluctantly drops off the spoon. Don't add all the egg unless needed.

To make the cream filling, beat the egg yolks and caster sugar for a few minutes until pale and slightly thickened. Whisk in the cornflour and plain flour.

Heat the milk in a small saucepan until just boiling, then pour onto the egg mixture and whisk well. Return the mixture to the saucepan and stir over a low heat until thick and creamy. Transfer to a bowl and place cling film directly onto the surface of the pastry cream, then cool and chill until later.

Preheat the oven to 200°C. Line two baking trays with baking parchment and place our eclair template underneath the paper (scan the QR code to download). Spoon the choux mixture into a piping bag and, if necessary, cut off the tip so the opening is 2cm wide. Following the template, pipe lines onto the baking parchment - there should be six 10cm-long eclairs per tray. Repeat until the mixture is used up and use a damp finger to flatten any peaks in the choux.

Bake for 25 minutes, reducing the temperature to 180°C fan as soon as they go in the oven. After 25 minutes, remove from the oven and turn off the heat. Carefully use a cocktail stick to poke three holes in the underside of each bun to allow any steam to escape. Return to the oven, upside-down, to dry out for 5 minutes until crisp and golden. Remove and set aside to cool.

Meanwhile, finish the cream filling. Add 50ml of water to the freeze-dried raspberries, if using, and leave to soak for 5 minutes. Using a fork, squash the soaked or fresh raspberries and then sieve the liquid, setting aside the raspberry juice for the icing. Gently fold the raspberries into the cream filling and spoon into a piping bag. Slice each bun lengthwise along the side, being careful not to cut all the way through, then pipe the raspberry cream into each cooled bun.

For the icing, add the raspberry juice to the icing sugar, a little at a time, and mix until smooth and the consistency of golden syrup. Arrange the eclairs on a wire rack, decorate with the icing, and allow to set.

Melt the white chocolate in a microwavable bowl in 30-second bursts until runny, then drizzle it over the eclairs. Chop the dried raspberries and sprinkle them over each eclair, or top each with a whole fresh raspberry.

BAKER'S TIP

Use clean scissors to cut the choux from the tip of the bag after piping each line for a neat finish.

Scan for template

MUM'S SCONES

Mum has never been one to throw anything away, and she has even been known to freeze sour milk until she has a spare few minutes to whip up a batch of these delicious scones. They can be made with non-sour milk, but they will not be quite as fluffy and delicious. For added dimension, try adding chopped glacé cherries, crystallised ginger, sultanas, raisins, or chocolate chips. Top with the classic cream and jam (ALWAYS cream first!), fruit curd, butter, or even cheese.

Makes: 16
Prep time: 25 minutes
Cooking time: 8-10 minutes
Oven temp: 200°C fan

110g unsalted butter
450g self-raising flour
1 tsp salt
55g caster sugar
285ml milk or sour milk

Rub the butter into the flour and salt using your fingers. When combined, add the sugar and stir thoroughly.

Add the milk a little at a time, mixing with a palette knife or spoon until it forms a soft dough. Turn out onto a lightly floured surface and knead for 3 to 4 minutes. If the dough is very sticky, add a little more flour until the dough is rollable.

Roll the dough until 1-2cm thick, depending on how chunky you like your scones! Using a cookie cutter or a knife and a glass as a guide, cut into circles approximately 6cm in diameter. Keep re-rolling until you have used all the dough.

Put the scones on a baking tray 6-8cm apart. Bake for 8 to 10 minutes until golden brown.

MUM'S TIP

To make delicious savoury scones, replace the sugar with 125g strong grated cheese and 1 teaspoon of mustard powder.

MUM'S FLAPJACK

I've always had a sweet tooth, but if I'm ever under the weather then I always crave Mum's flapjack, and it's the first thing I ate after giving birth to all three of my children. It's slightly sticky, chewy at the edges, and just delicious. It keeps well in an airtight tin and makes a wonderful treat at the top of a windy mountain or with a cup of tea in front of a roaring fire. It should be a staple in every household which is why we are generously sharing this trusty recipe with you.

Makes: 15
Prep time: 15 minutes
Cooking time: 20 minutes
Oven temp: 160°C fan

225g butter
225g demerara sugar
1 heaped tbsp golden syrup
340g porridge oats

Grease and line the bottom of an 20x20cm baking tin with baking parchment.

Heat the butter, sugar and golden syrup in a large saucepan over a medium heat. Stir continuously until the butter has melted and the sugar has dissolved.

Remove from the heat, add the oats, and stir until well combined. All the oats should have a good covering of the syrupy mixture – if it is very wet, add more oats, a little at a time, mixing well each time.

Tip into the tin and, using the back of a spoon, make sure the flapjack is level and evenly spread out.

Bake for 20 minutes or until golden brown. Once baked, remove from the oven and leave in the tin to cool before cutting into squares.

MUM'S TIP
Be generous with the syrup; it will work with less but it won't be as sticky or scrumptious.

ALMOND AND CHOCOLATE CROISSANTS

When I first spotted these in a French bakery, I was delighted. They combine the best of a pain au chocolat and an almond croissant. I can't imagine a better breakfast than a warm, home-baked croissant with a cup of coffee and some fresh berries. They take some time to make, but they are absolutely worth it. Double the recipe if you'd like some spare!

Makes: 6
Prep time: 1 hour 45 minutes, plus 18 hours proving/chilling
Cooking time: 20 minutes
Oven temp: 180°C fan

FOR THE MARZIPAN FILLING

40g ground almonds

20g icing sugar

30g caster sugar

1 tsp egg white or water

FOR THE DOUGH

300g strong white bread flour

1 tsp salt

30g caster sugar

180ml cold water

7g instant yeast

180g room temperature butter

FOR THE CHOCOLATE FILLING

50g dark chocolate, cut into 1cm-wide pieces, or 12 chocolate batons

FOR THE TOPPING

1 egg, beaten, to glaze (or use plant-based milk)

2 tbsp flaked almonds

10g icing sugar, to dust

To make the marzipan, place all the ingredients in a food processor and blitz until they form a soft dough. Add more egg white or water if needed. Wrap in reusable food wrap and chill in the fridge ready to fill the croissants.

To make the dough, combine the flour, salt and sugar in a mixing bowl. Mix the water and yeast together in a jug until fully dissolved, then make a well in the dry ingredients and pour in the yeasty liquid. Stir until it forms a rough dough.

Place the dough on a floured surface and knead for 10 minutes. Shape into a ball, place in a lightly oiled bowl, cover with a clean shower cap, and chill in the fridge for 2 hours.

Meanwhile, put the butter between two sheets of baking parchment and use a rolling pin to bash and roll it out - take your time as it's important to break down the butter. Shape the butter into a rectangle, about 20x15cm, and place it in the fridge to chill.

Tip the chilled dough onto a floured work surface and roll it out into a rectangle about 40x20cm. Shape the corners by pulling the dough out with your hands, but if the dough shrinks back to an oval, pop it back in the fridge for 10 minutes before trying again. When shaped, place the unwrapped slab of butter into the centre of the dough, covering the middle third.

Fold one side of the dough up and halfway over the butter. Then, take the other side and fold it over the butter so that the edges meet in the middle and the butter is fully enclosed. Fold in half along the line where the dough meets, then wrap in reusable food wrap and return to the fridge for 30 minutes.

Repeat the rolling, folding and chilling process twice more - rolling the dough while it is still folded, without adding more butter. If the butter breaks through the surface of the dough at any point, don't worry – just dust it with a little flour and continue. After the third fold, wrap it in reusable food wrap and chill in the fridge overnight. At this stage, the dough should have 81 layers.

The next day, carefully roll the dough out into a rectangle, about 50x25cm. Neatly trim the edges with a sharp knife, then cut the dough into six even rectangles.

Cut the marzipan into six equal pieces and roll it into sausage shapes, about 1cm shorter than the shortest edge of your rectangles. Place the chocolate about 2cm in from one of the shorter sides of a pastry rectangle, parallel with the rectangle's edge, then place a marzipan roll next to the chocolate.

Gently roll the croissant up, encasing the chocolate and marzipan. Once covered, add more chocolate and continue to roll the pastry. Be careful not to press too hard and crush the delicate layers.

Place the rolled croissant, fold side down, on a lined baking tray. Repeat with the remaining rectangles.

Leave plenty of space between each croissant to allow room to rise. Cover with a damp tea towel and leave to rise for 2 hours, ideally at 18°C to 24°C. Place in the fridge for a further 30 minutes to chill before baking.

Generously glaze each croissant with beaten egg and sprinkle with flaked almonds. Bake in the centre of the oven for 20 minutes until risen and golden brown. Remove from the oven and cool on a wire rack. Use a sieve to liberally dust the croissants with icing sugar.

GRANDMA BUN'S FUDGE

Grandma had a neat grey bun when I was little, and even though she'd cut it off by the time I was about four, she remained Grandma Bun for the rest of her life. She was my mum's mum and a great baker, and she would make this fudge as a treat for us on our birthdays. We would beg her to make it in between as well, but she usually made us wait. Perhaps there can be too much of a good thing, but I for one can't stop at one, two, or even three pieces!

Makes: 30 pieces
Prep time: 5 minutes
Cooking time: 1 hour

1 x 410g tin of evaporated milk
125g butter
450g caster sugar
1 tsp vanilla extract
1 piece of chocolate of your choice (optional)

FOR THE TOPPING (OPTIONAL)
100g chocolate of your choice

Place a glass of cold water in the fridge – this will be used to test the fudge later on – and grease a 20x20cm baking tin.

Add the evaporated milk and butter to a saucepan over a low heat and stir constantly until the butter has melted. Add the sugar and stir constantly for 15 to 20 minutes until the fudge starts to thicken, bubble and turn light brown. Don't be tempted to stop stirring or it will burn!

To test the fudge, drop a small amount into the cold water. If it is ready, it will form a soft ball. Keep stirring and bubbling away until you are certain it forms a soft ball – this may take up to 35 minutes. Don't be tempted to stop until you're certain!

When ready, take the fudge off the heat and beat in the vanilla and a piece of chocolate (if using) until the fudge starts to thicken, then pour it into the prepared tray and leave to cool.

For added decadence, pour your choice of melted chocolate over the top.

BAKER'S TIP
This fudge is also delicious with chopped nuts or dried fruit stirred in at the last stage – add whatever takes your fancy!

RHUBARB AND CUSTARD DOUGHNUTS

A classic combination of nostalgic flavours in a freshly baked doughnut is a huge treat. You could always cheat and buy fresh custard if you'd like to save some time – these doughnuts will still be a delight.

Makes: 8-9
Prep time: 1 hour 35 minutes, plus 1 hour 20 minutes proving/chilling
Cooking time: 1 hour 5 minutes

FOR THE CUSTARD FILLING

3 egg yolks

50g light soft brown sugar

15g cornflour

150ml milk

½ tsp vanilla extract

10g butter, room temperature

FOR THE DOUGHNUTS

1 tsp instant yeast

120ml lukewarm milk

1½ tbsp light soft brown sugar

280g plain flour

½ tsp salt

2 tsp ground ginger

1 egg

20g golden syrup

45g butter, softened

750ml sunflower oil, for frying

50g granulated sugar, to coat

FOR THE RHUBARB COMPOTE

125g fresh rhubarb stalks

25g caster sugar

½ tsp vanilla extract

1 tbsp water

YOU WILL NEED

2 piping bags with 1cm tips

To make the custard filling, whisk together the egg yolks, brown sugar and cornflour in a large bowl.

Combine the milk and vanilla extract in a small pan and warm through until it starts to bubble gently at the sides. Remove from the heat and pour half of the milk into the bowl of egg yolk mixture, whisking briskly for 30 seconds. Transfer the egg mixture back to the pan with the remaining milk and heat over a medium heat, whisking constantly, until very thick.

Remove from the heat and stir in the butter until fully combined. Leave to stand for 10 minutes, whisking every so often, then transfer to a bowl and leave to cool. Place a piece of cling film directly on the surface of the custard to prevent a skin forming, then place it in the fridge to chill until you are ready to fill the doughnuts.

To make the doughnuts, start by combining the yeast, warm milk and half of the brown sugar in a jug. Leave to stand for about 10 minutes, until foamy.

In a large bowl, or the bowl of a stand mixer with the dough hook attached, combine the flour, salt, ginger, and the remaining brown sugar. Add the egg, golden syrup, and yeast mixture to the bowl and mix until the dough comes together. Increase the speed to medium and mix for a further 10 minutes, or knead by hand until you have soft, smooth dough.

Gradually add the softened butter to the dough, ensuring the last piece is fully combined before adding another. If you are working by hand this may take a little longer, but persist, it will come together! Once the butter is incorporated, continue to knead for 5 minutes to form a very soft, smooth dough. Transfer the dough to an oiled bowl and cover with a damp tea towel or a reusable bowl cover. Leave in a warm place to rise for about 1 hour.

Meanwhile, prepare the compote by chopping the rhubarb into rough pieces, about 2cm long. Place the rhubarb, caster sugar, vanilla extract, and water in a small pan over a low heat for about 20 minutes, stirring regularly, until the rhubarb has completely broken down and you have a thick, sticky compote. Transfer to a bowl and leave to cool until you are ready to fill the doughnuts.

Once risen, turn the dough out onto a floured surface and roll out to about 2cm thick, then cover with a damp tea towel and leave to rest for 5 minutes. Using a 6cm cookie cutter, or the rim of a glass, cut out as many circles as you can. Place the circles on a baking tray lined with baking parchment. Cover with a damp tea towel and leave to rise for a further 20 minutes.

In preparation for frying, put the granulated sugar in a bowl ready to coat the doughnuts and place a wire rack over a baking tray to collect the oil as it drains. Heat the sunflower oil in a large pan to about 175°C.

Once the oil is at temperature, gently lower the doughnuts into the pan using a slotted spoon. Cook in batches of two for 1 and a half to 2 minutes each side until they are an even golden-brown colour. Remove from the oil and place on the wire rack for about 30 seconds before tossing in the sugar. Repeat the process with the remaining doughnuts and leave to cool completely on the rack. Using your finger, poke a hole in each doughnut, opening it up a little inside to make room for the filling.

Put the chilled custard and rhubarb compote in separate piping bags and, if necessary, snip about 1cm off the tip. Half fill the middle of each doughnut, first with rhubarb, then with a generous helping of custard. These are best enjoyed the same day, however they can be kept in the fridge in an airtight container to be enjoyed the following day. Just bring them back up to room temperature and give them a fresh sprinkling of sugar before serving. Enjoy!

TIFFIN

This is a really adaptable recipe that helps you turn old or broken cake and/or biscuits into something really delicious. Try out different flavour combinations to suit your taste; why not try dark chocolate with pieces of crystallised ginger, or use white chocolate and add cranberries?

Serves: 12
Prep time: 25 minutes, plus 2-3 hours chilling

FOR THE TIFFIN

200g dark chocolate

250g butter, cubed

500g leftover cake (approx.)

6-8 biscuits, bashed into chunks

50g fruit or nuts of your choice (for example, sultanas, cranberries, walnuts, glacé cherries, and crystallised or stem ginger)

FOR THE TOPPING

200g milk chocolate

Lightly grease a tin, approximately 30x20cm, and line it with a silicone sheet or baking parchment. This tiffin can be made in any shape tin you like, so use whichever you have to hand.

Melt the chocolate and butter together and stir until well combined. Break the cake into crumbs, then stir it into the melted chocolate. Add the biscuits, your choice of dried fruit and nuts, and stir well. Transfer the mixture to the tin and pat it down with a spatula until level.

If using, melt the chocolate for the topping and pour it over the top of the tiffin, spreading it out evenly to the edges. Chill in the fridge for 2 to 3 hours, then cut into 12 squares.

This is best stored in the fridge where it will last for several days.

BAKER'S TIP

You can also add your favourite chocolates, such as any you might have left over from Easter (if you're lucky!) – Crunchie bars and Maltesers work really well in tiffin.

DOMINIC'S TRIPLE CHOCOLATE COOKIES

Dominic, my brother, says: "These cookies have quickly become a firm family favourite and I love baking them with the nieces and nephews. The best bit is you can use almost any chocolate and they still work well – it's great fun to experiment with different flavour combinations!"

Makes: 20
Prep time: 15 minutes
Cooking time: 10-12 minutes
Oven temp: 175°C fan

115g butter, softened

100g caster sugar

110g light soft brown sugar

1 egg

1 tsp vanilla extract

65g plain flour

30g cocoa powder

½ tsp bicarbonate of soda

50g milk chocolate, roughly chopped

50g caramel-filled milk chocolate, roughly chopped

50g orange-flavoured chocolate, roughly chopped

In a large bowl, use an electric mixer to beat the softened butter, caster sugar and brown sugar until light and fluffy. Beat in the egg and vanilla extract until well combined.

Gradually add the flour, cocoa powder, and bicarbonate of soda, mixing until just combined, then gently fold in all the chopped chocolate.

Line a baking tray with a reusable silicone sheet or baking parchment. Scoop out tablespoon-sized portions of the dough (approximately 30g each) and place them on the prepared baking tray, spacing them about 5cm apart and flattening them slightly with your hand. You may need to bake a few batches to use all the dough.

Bake the cookies for 10 to 12 minutes or until the edges are set but the centres are still soft. Rotate the baking sheet halfway through for even baking.

Let the cookies cool on the baking sheet for a few minutes before transferring them to a wire rack to cool completely.

DOM'S TIP

Make sure you leave room on the baking tray for these to spread during baking.

Add a sprinkle of flaky sea salt after baking for a more grown-up taste.

DAN'S FRUIT CRUMBLE

Dan, my brother says: "This recipe always reminds me of my parents' wonderful vegetable patch and all the fun times we had in their garden. It brings out the best of the rhubarb's flavour and is a wonderful treat for when the cold sting of winter is still lingering. The zing of the orange pairs beautifully with the tartness of the rhubarb, the stem ginger adds a warm spice, and the oats give the crumble a lovely texture."

Serves: 8-10
Prep time: 20 minutes
Cooking time: 45 minutes
Oven temp: 160°C fan

FOR THE FILLING

800g fresh rhubarb stalks, trimmed and cut into 1.5-inch pieces, or any fruit of your choice

100g caster sugar (adjust to taste)

3 large oranges, zested and juiced

1 tsp vanilla extract

FOR THE CRUMBLE

100g cold butter, diced

150g plain flour

100g rolled oats

100g demerara sugar

3 cubes stem ginger (in syrup), finely chopped

2 tbsp stem ginger syrup (from the same jar as above)

Combine the rhubarb, caster sugar, orange zest, orange juice, and vanilla extract in an ovenproof dish, approximately 30x20cm. Spread it out evenly, then bake for 15 minutes to cook the fruit down a little.

To make the crumble, add the butter and flour to a mixing bowl. Rub the butter into the flour using your fingertips until it resembles coarse breadcrumbs. Stir in the oats and demerara sugar. Stir in the chopped stem ginger and 2 tbsp of the ginger syrup for a spicy, fragrant kick.

Once the fruit has baked for 15 minutes, flatten it with a spoon then sprinkle the crumble mixture evenly over the top, making sure it's well covered. Bake for a further 30 minutes until the topping is golden brown and the fruit is bubbling up at the edges.

Remove from the oven and let it cool for a few minutes before serving with custard, clotted cream, or vanilla ice cream for an extra treat.

DAN'S TIP

For extra crunch, you can add a handful of chopped hazelnuts or almonds to the crumble mixture. If you prefer a tarter crumble, reduce the sugar in the filling to 75g.

RHIANNON'S CARAMEL SHORTBREAD

Rhiannon, my youngest sister, says: "This caramel shortbread recipe has been a Honeywell family favourite ever since I perfected it as a teenager to celebrate my brother's engagement. Now, no family gathering is complete without it. Choose your favourite chocolate to top it off, and don't hold back on the caramel and chocolate — getting that perfect ratio is key!"
Enjoy, but be warned: once you've had one slice, you'll definitely be coming back for more!

Makes: 24
Prep time: 45 minutes
Cooking time: 1 hour 20 minutes
Oven temp: 160°C fan

FOR THE SHORTBREAD

230g cold, salted butter, cubed
340g plain flour
110g caster sugar

FOR THE CARAMEL

1 x 397g tin of condensed milk
170g butter
85g caster sugar
3 tbsp golden syrup

FOR THE TOPPING

500g chocolate of your choice, chopped or broken into pieces
50g white chocolate

YOU WILL NEED

A piping bag with a 5mm tip

Lightly grease a 30x20cm baking tray with butter. Then, in a large mixing bowl, rub the butter into the flour using your fingertips until it resembles breadcrumbs. It can take a few minutes but be patient! Stir in the sugar then knead and bring it together with your hands until it forms a dough.

Break off pieces of dough and gradually fill the bottom of the baking tray. Pat the shortbread dough down with your fingers then smooth it with the back of a spoon. Prick all over with a fork before baking for 40 minutes until golden brown.

Allow the shortbread to cool completely while you make the caramel. Add the condensed milk, butter, sugar and syrup to a heavy-bottomed saucepan and place over a low heat, stirring constantly. Allow to bubble for a few minutes but don't be tempted to stop stirring or else it will burn! Remove from the heat and test the caramel by dropping a small blob from the wooden spoon into a glass of cold water. If it forms a ball, it's ready. If not, return it to the heat and test again in a few minutes.

Pour the caramel onto the shortbread and spread it out evenly. Set aside and allow to cool completely. Once cooled, add your chocolate of choice to a heatproof bowl, place it over a pan of simmering water, and stir until melted. Melt the white chocolate in the same way (in a separate bowl) and add it to a piping bag. Use a peg or clip to keep the piping end sealed until you are ready to use it as the chocolate will be runny.

Pour the bowl of melted chocolate over the cooled caramel and spread it evenly over the whole pan. Immediately pipe evenly spaced lines of chocolate widthways across the chocolate.

Using a cocktail stick, pull the white chocolate lengthways through the milk chocolate, and then back up again. Repeat until you have a feathered pattern, then allow to cool before slicing with a sharp knife.

RHIANNON'S TIP

For a beautiful finish, try piping small circles of white chocolate onto the melted chocolate layer and using a cocktail stick to gently drag them to create delicate hearts.

RHUBARB HAZELNUT TARTLET

A sweet, pretty tart that makes a great dessert. Serve warm with a dollop of ice cream or crème fraîche, or cold with a cup of tea. For a quick swap, replace the hazelnuts with ground almonds. This recipe uses two eggs: beat them together, set aside 35g for the dough, then use the remaining for the filling.

Makes: 4 mini tartlets or 1 large 9-inch tart
Prep time: 35 minutes, plus 1 hour chilling
Cooking time: 1 hour 15 minutes
Oven temp: Pastry case: 180°C fan;
Filling: 160°C fan

FOR THE DOUGH

40g roasted hazelnuts

120g plain flour

40g caster sugar

¼ tsp salt

60g cold butter, cubed

35g beaten egg

FOR THE FILLING

75g butter, softened

75g caster sugar

¼ tsp salt

50g beaten egg

100g roasted hazelnuts

1 tbsp plain flour

FOR THE TOPPING

3 fresh rhubarb stalks

½ tbsp caster sugar

In a food processor, finely grind the hazelnuts to the consistency of breadcrumbs. Place the ground nuts in a mixing bowl and combine with the flour, sugar and salt.

Rub the butter into the mixture using the tips of your fingers to form an even, crumbly texture. Add the beaten egg and quickly mix to create a soft dough - avoid kneading and overworking the pastry.

Grease four individual tartlet tins or 1 large 9-inch tart tin. Roll out the pastry on a lightly floured surface and place in the prepared tin/s, gently pressing into the corners. Prick the base a few times with a fork, then cover with reusable food wrap and chill for half an hour.

Remove the chilled pastry cases from the fridge and uncover. Place a sheet of baking parchment over the pastry, top with baking beans or rice, and blind bake the bases at 180°C fan for 15 minutes. Remove from the oven and leave to cool. Gently tip out the rice or beans, making sure to set them aside for your next bake.

Meanwhile, prepare the filling. Whisk together the butter, sugar, salt and egg until the mixture is light and smooth. Blitz the hazelnuts in a food processor until smooth and creamy, like peanut butter. This can take some time but be patient! Add the hazelnut paste and flour to the wet mixture and stir until well combined.

Cut the rhubarb stalks in half lengthwise then slice diagonally into small pieces, about 1-inch long. Pour the nut filling into the pastry case/s and spread it out evenly, leaving a little space to prevent the tarts overflowing as they bake. Arrange the rhubarb in a diamond pattern on top of the filling and sprinkle over the caster sugar.

Reduce the oven temperature to 160°C fan and bake the tart/s for approximately 1 hour, until golden brown and no longer wobbly. Note, a larger tart will take longer to bake than the smaller ones. Leave to cool completely in the tin/s before carefully removing.

BAKER'S TIP

Other fruits work well in the recipe, just make sure they're not too wet. We recommend apricots, peaches, or nectarines.

EARL GREY TEA AND LEMON CAKES

The gentle, classic flavours of Earl Grey and lemon combine to make these delicate cakes that are simple to make but still a showstopper. It goes without saying that they are best enjoyed with a steaming cup of tea.

Makes: 6
Prep time: 45 minutes, plus 20 minutes cooling
Cooking time: 20-25 minutes
Oven temp: 160°C fan

FOR THE CAKES

75ml milk

2 Earl Grey tea bags

½ tsp vanilla extract

120g butter, softened

120g caster sugar

1 egg

170g plain flour

1 tsp baking powder

FOR THE TOPPING

1 tbsp lemon juice

100g icing sugar

Pressed or fresh edible flowers, such as violas and pansies

Grease six holes of a muffin tin and dust with flour. Tap out any excess flour and use it for the cake batter.

In a small pan, combine the milk, tea bags and vanilla extract. Warm over a medium heat until the milk starts to bubble at the sides. Remove from the heat and leave to cool and infuse for 15 minutes. Squeeze out any liquid from the teabags before discarding.

In a mixing bowl, beat the butter and sugar until light and creamy. Add the egg and mix until well combined. Add the flour, baking powder and tea mixture. Whisk together until you have a smooth, thick batter.

Using a spoon, divide the batter evenly between the prepared muffin tin holes. Bake for 20 to 25 minutes until golden and a cocktail stick inserted into the centre of a cake comes out clean.

Leave to cool in the tin for 5 minutes before removing and leaving to cool completely on a wire rack.

Once cooled, return the cakes to the tin and, using the tin as guide, carefully cut the top off each with a sharp knife. This flat surface will become the bottom of your cakes when turned over (and yes, you can eat the scraps!). Return the cakes, cut side down, to the wire rack ready for icing.

In a small bowl, add the lemon juice to the icing sugar, a little at a time, until it's the consistency of golden syrup.

Spoon the icing over the top of each cake, allowing a little to drip down the sides. Finish each cake with an edible flower and serve. These pretty treats are perfect for a picnic or afternoon tea with friends. Enjoy!

BAKER'S TIP

You can press your own edible flowers to use as decorations. Only pick flowers on a dry day and ensure you are confident they are both edible and free from pesticides. Press between sheets of baking parchment in a flower press or between heavy books for a few days. If you're short of time, you can use fresh flowers as decorations, too. They won't stay fresh for long, so decorate the cakes just before you eat them.

SFOUF CAKE

Sfouf is a Lebanese cake traditionally made with semolina, turmeric and sesame paste. Naturally egg free, this flavoursome cake is risen with baking powder. It is also easily made vegan by opting for a plant-based milk alternative. Not as sweet as a vanilla sponge, this bright and sunny cake is perfect for brunch.

Serves: 9
Prep time: 15 minutes
Cooking time: 30 minutes
Oven temp: 180°C fan

FOR THE CAKE

120g plain flour

120g semolina flour

1 ¼ tsp turmeric

1 tsp baking powder

185g caster sugar

185ml milk

75ml sunflower oil

FOR THE TOPPING

1 tsp black sesame seeds

1 tsp white sesame seeds (optional)

1 tsp pearl sugar (optional)

Grease a 20x20cm baking tin and dust it well with plain flour by adding a tablespoon or so to the tin and tapping and rotating until the base and sides are covered.

In a mixing bowl, whisk the plain flour, semolina flour, turmeric, baking powder and caster sugar until combined.

Make a well in the centre of the dry ingredients and add the milk and sunflower oil. Mix until you have a smooth batter.

Pour the batter into the prepared tin. Evenly scatter the sesame seeds and pearl sugar over the surface of the cake, if using.

Bake for 30 minutes or until a cocktail stick inserted into the middle of the cake comes out clean. Allow the cake to cool for 10 minutes before removing from the tin and cutting into nine equal squares. Best served slightly warm, this cake is perfect with a cup of coffee. Enjoy!

SPICED ICED BUNS

A twist on a childhood favourite, these buns combine fresh, sweet dough with a sticky icing topping. Elevate them by adding fresh or dried edible flowers. If using fresh flowers as decorations, ice them just before serving.

Makes: 6
Prep time: 45 minutes, plus 2 hours proving
Cooking time: 15-20 minutes
Oven temp: 180°C fan

FOR THE DOUGH

50g raisins

½ tsp mixed spice

2 tbsp water

125g strong white bread flour

125g plain flour

1 tsp instant yeast

½ tsp salt

25g salted butter, melted

1 tbsp caster sugar

100ml warm milk

1 small egg

FOR THE ICING

100g icing sugar

1½ tbsp milk

Edible dried or fresh flowers (see Baker's Tip)

Add the raisins, mixed spice, and 2 tablespoons of water to a small pan and place over a medium heat. Cook for a few minutes until the liquid has evaporated and the raisins have plumped up. Remove from the heat and set aside to cool.

Empty both flours into a mixing bowl and add the yeast and salt to opposite sides of the bowl. Make a well in the centre, then add the butter, sugar, milk and egg. Gradually bring the ingredients together using a wooden spoon until you have a soft, sticky dough.

If you have a stand mixer, use the dough hook attachment to mix the dough on a medium speed for 5 to 10 minutes. Otherwise, tip the dough onto a lightly floured surface and knead well for 10 to 15 minutes until the dough is smooth and elastic.

Add the spiced raisins to the dough and knead for a few more minutes until the fruit is evenly distributed throughout the dough. Roll the dough into a ball and place it in a lightly oiled bowl. Cover with a clean, damp tea towel or a clean shower cap and leave in a warm place to rise for an hour or until the dough has doubled in size.

Divide the dough into six equal pieces. Roll the dough into sausage shapes, tucking the ends under. Place on a baking tray lined with baking parchment, leaving a 2cm gap between each bun.

Cover the buns with a damp tea towel, then leave to prove in a warm place for about 1 hour or until doubled in size.

Bake for 10 to 15 minutes until risen and golden, then transfer to a wire rack to cool.

In a small bowl, combine the icing sugar and milk until thick and smooth. Spoon over the cooled buns and finish with edible flowers.

BAKER'S TIP

Edible flowers include citrus blossom, daisies, dandelions, hibiscus, honeysuckle, lavender, lilac, pansies, roses and violets. Only pick flowers on a dry day and ensure you are confident they are both edible and free from pesticides.

SPICED EASTER EGG BISCUITS

These lightly spiced biscuits are filled with a homemade orange curd that can be whipped up in under 20 minutes, with any leftovers being stored in the fridge ready to be lovingly spread over toasted hot cross buns. If you love hot cross buns and the smell of warming spices filling up the kitchen, it's definitely time to try these!

Makes: 8
Prep time: 50 minutes, plus 30 minutes chilling
Cooking time: 20 minutes
Oven temp: 160°C fan

FOR THE BISCUITS

150g plain flour

1½ tsp mixed spice

20g cornflour

80g unsalted butter, cubed

75g caster sugar

1 egg, beaten

Icing sugar, for dusting

FOR THE ORANGE CURD

2 egg yolks

70g caster sugar

1 large orange, zested and juiced

20g cold, unsalted butter

YOU WILL NEED

Egg-shaped cookie cutter or template

Combine the plain flour, mixed spice, and cornflour in a bowl, then tip in the butter and sugar. Use your fingertips to rub the butter into the flour mixture until it resembles breadcrumbs.

Gradually add the beaten egg, mixing until it forms a dough. Form the dough into a ball, wrap in reusable food wrap, and place in the fridge for 30 minutes to chill. This will stop the biscuits from spreading when you bake them, helping them keep their shape.

Whilst the dough is chilling, make the orange curd. In a saucepan (no heat), whisk the egg yolks and caster sugar together until smooth. Add the zest and juice of the orange and whisk until combined.

Turn to a low-medium heat and cook slowly, stirring continuously with a wooden spoon until the curd is thick enough to coat the back of a spoon.

Remove from the heat and whisk in the cold butter, a little at a time, until it forms a smooth, glossy curd. Leave to cool in the saucepan.

Once the dough has chilled, lightly dust a work surface with flour and roll it out until the dough is about the thickness of a £1 coin. Using an 8cm egg-shaped cutter (or scan the QR code to download our template), cut out 16 egg-shaped biscuits. You will need to re-roll the off-cuts to get all 16 biscuits.

Using a 3cm circle cutter (or the lid of a bottle if you haven't got one), cut a circle out of half of the biscuits. These will be the 'yolk holes' for the biscuit toppers.

Line a baking tray with baking parchment and arrange the biscuits, leaving gaps in between (bake in batches if needed). Bake the biscuits for 10 minutes or until they are uniform in colour and firm to the touch. Remove the baked biscuits from the oven and let them cool completely on a wire rack.

FOR THE ASSEMBLY

Lay the egg biscuits with the 'yolk holes' on a sheet of baking parchment and lightly dust with icing sugar to turn them white. Add a spoonful of curd onto the eight remaining biscuits and spread it out to the edges.

Carefully sandwich the dusted biscuits on top of the curd-topped biscuit so the curd (or yolk) pokes through the hole, then arrange them on a plate. Devour and enjoy!

BAKER'S TIP

Lemon curd (see page 62) also works well in this recipe, and you can also use shop-bought fruit curd. Save your egg whites for meringues!

Scan for template

DOUBLE CHOCOLATE HOT CROSS BUN LOAF

As long as you're not a hot cross bun purist, you'll love this lightly spiced, chocolatey loaf. I first baked it for my daughter as she doesn't like raisins, and in our house it's barely out of the oven before little (and big) hands reach for a slice, or even a whole 'bun'! If you prefer a traditional hot cross bun, swap out the chocolate for raisins and add a white cross, made from 1 tablespoon of plain flour and enough water to make a paste, just before you bake them instead of the white chocolate cross.

Makes: 1 loaf
Prep time: 1 hour, plus 1 hour 45 minutes proving
Cooking time: 20-25 minutes
Oven temp: 180°C fan

FOR THE DOUGH

1 tsp instant yeast
125ml lukewarm milk
50g caster sugar
300g strong white bread flour
1½ tsp mixed spice
½ tsp salt
50g butter, melted
1 medium egg, plus extra for glazing
60g dark chocolate, roughly chopped

FOR THE TOPPING

40g white chocolate

YOU WILL NEED

Piping bag or bottle with a small tip

Start by mixing the yeast, warm milk and 1 teaspoon of caster sugar in a jug. Leave to stand for 10 minutes or until foamy.

In a large bowl, or the bowl of a stand mixer with a dough hook attached, combine the flour, mixed spice, salt and remaining sugar. Add the melted butter, egg and yeast mixture to the bowl and mix to form a dough. If using a stand mixer, increase the speed to medium and mix for a further 10 minutes; if mixing by hand, knead until you have a soft, smooth dough.

Transfer the dough to a lightly oiled bowl and cover with a clean, damp tea towel (or a clean shower cap). Leave in a warm place to rise for 1 hour or until doubled in size. Meanwhile, prepare a 2lb loaf tin by greasing and lining with baking parchment.

Once risen, turn the dough out onto a floured surface, add the dark chocolate, and knead for 1 minute to combine. Divide the dough into eight equal portions, then form each portion into a neat ball and arrange them in the prepared loaf tin. Cover and leave to rise again for 45 minutes or until doubled in size.

Gently brush the loaf with beaten egg and bake in the oven for 20 to 25 minutes, covering with foil if the bread begins to darken too much. The bread is baked once its base sounds hollow when tapped. Leave the loaf in the tin for 10 minutes before removing it and transferring to a wire rack to cool.

Melt the white chocolate in a bowl over a pan of simmering water before transferring to a piping bag or bottle with a small tip. Pipe a cross on the surface of each bun. Slice the loaf to serve.

BAKER'S TIP

If your yeast is out of date, there's no need to throw it out. Test it's still active by adding 1 teaspoon to some warm water with a half a teaspoon of sugar and waiting 10 minutes. If the yeast bubbles and foams, it will work in your recipe. If not, use new yeast.

You can swap instant yeast for fresh yeast; just use double the weight of fresh yeast vs. instant. For example, if a recipe calls for 7g of instant yeast, use 14g of fresh.

HOT CROSS BUN WREATH

It's not Easter without a hot cross bun, and by arranging them in a circle you have an instant table centrepiece. Dipped in the spiced butter, you won't be able to stop yourself from eating the whole thing! This recipe is easy to adapt, so why not try swapping the raisins for small chocolate pieces!

Makes: 12 buns (1 wreath)
Prep time: 55 minutes, plus 2 hours proving
Cooking time: 25-30 minutes
Oven temp: 180°C fan

FOR THE DOUGH

265g strong white bread flour

1 tbsp instant yeast

50g caster sugar

1 tsp mixed spice

½ tsp salt

50g butter, melted

1 egg

125ml milk

60g raisins

FOR THE CROSSES

2 tbsp plain flour

1 tsp water

FOR THE SPICED BUTTER

100g butter, softened

2 tbsp light soft brown sugar

2 tsp ground cinnamon

FOR THE GLAZE

1 tbsp apricot jam

1 tbsp hot water

YOU WILL NEED

Piping bag or bottle with a small tip

Add the flour, yeast, sugar, and mixed spice to a bowl and mix until combined.

In a measuring jug, whisk together the salt, melted butter, egg, and milk then pour into the dry ingredients. Mix until a sticky, soft dough forms.

Turn the dough out onto a floured surface and knead for 10 minutes.

Place the dough into a bowl, cover with a clean shower cap or a damp tea towel, and leave in a warm place to prove for 1 hour.

Remove from the bowl and knead in the raisins. Return to the bowl, cover again, and prove for another 30 minutes.

Line a large baking tray or round ovenproof dish with baking parchment.

Form 12 even dough balls, roughly 40g each, and place on the prepared baking tray in a large circle.

For the crosses, mix the flour and a little water to form a thick paste, the consistency of toothpaste. Spoon the mixture into a piping bag and snip about 5mm off the tip of the bag. Pipe a cross onto each of the buns.

Leave to prove for another 30 minutes, then bake in the oven for 25 to 30 minutes until the hot cross buns are golden brown.

While the wreath bakes, prepare the spiced butter. Combine the butter, brown sugar and cinnamon in a small bowl – ideally one that'll fit nicely into the centre of your wreath.

Once baked, remove the wreath from the oven and set aside. Prepare the glaze by combining the apricot jam and water in a small bowl then microwaving for about 15 seconds until melted. Use a pastry brush to glaze the buns while they're still hot, then leave them to cool slightly before serving with the spiced butter.

LEMON CURD

Versatile, tart and sweet, lemon curd is great when spread on a scone or a hot piece of buttered toast. It also makes a lovely tart when used as a filling with sweet pastry. Even in the fridge, it doesn't keep very long, but it will freeze well.

Makes: 3 standard jam jars (approx. 1kg)
Prep time: 15 minutes
Cooking time: 1 hour

450g cooking apples, peeled, cored and sliced

300g caster sugar

3 lemons, zested and juiced

100g butter

4 eggs, beaten and strained through a sieve

Cook the apples, without water, over a very low heat until soft. Keep stirring or they may burn. Once cooked, beat to a pulp before adding the sugar, lemon zest and juice, butter and eggs.

Stir continuously over a very low heat until the mixture thickens, approximately 20 to 30 minutes. Do not let the mixture boil.

When the curd has thickened, pour it into sterilised jars and pop on the lids. Once cooled, place in the fridge where it will keep unopened for about a month. It will also keep in the freezer for around 3 months unopened.

BAKER'S TIP

Keep the apple peels and cores for Apple Scrap Jelly on page 158.

FOOD IMPACT

"BIODIVERSITY IS ESSENTIAL FOR THE PROCESSES THAT SUPPORT ALL LIFE ON EARTH, INCLUDING HUMANS. WITHOUT A WIDE RANGE OF ANIMALS, PLANTS AND MICROORGANISMS, WE CANNOT HAVE THE HEALTHY ECOSYSTEMS THAT WE RELY ON TO PROVIDE US WITH THE AIR WE BREATHE AND THE FOOD WE EAT."

– THE ROYAL SOCIETY

WHAT'S THE PROBLEM?

Intensive farming is polluting our rivers, soils and bodies, and it is causing widespread biodiversity loss. 75% of the world's food is generated from only 12 plants and five animal species (source: Friends of the Earth), which means growing monocultures that usually require fertiliser and pesticides to grow. Pesticides harm bees and other wildlife, and fertilisers can lead to pollution in streams and rivers, killing fish and wildlife that rely on the water. However, there are now an increasing number of farmers that are farming in ways that nurture and regenerate soils and local ecosystems; this is often referred to as organic or regenerative farming.

WHAT CAN WE DO TO HELP?

CHOOSE ORGANIC OR REGENERATIVELY PRODUCED FOOD

A product that is certified organic has been assessed and verified as being grown using methods that benefit the land and human health rather than harm it. Organic farmers have to comply with strict regulations which ensures their farmers take care of the soil, ecosystems, animals, and people. This creates a natural balance between plants and animals to prevent and control pests and encourage birds, insects and other wildlife. To enable this system to thrive, crops are rotated and often a wider range of crop breeds are chosen to lower the risk of disease and increase soil and therefore plant health.

Regeneratively farmed food is similar in principle to organic but there is no set standard or certification. Farmers that call themselves regenerative do not till or plough the soil in order to maintain the soil structure. By keeping roots in the soil, the bacteria and fungi that are vital for soil and plant health are nourished. Animals are also often used to graze down crops after harvest and their manure acts as a natural fertiliser. This allows wildlife to thrive and the soil and land to regenerate and improve.

CONSIDER ANIMAL WELFARE

Think about animal welfare when buying eggs and dairy. Organic animals are free range and raised in conditions that allow them to behave more naturally. Inhumane practices such as beak trimming, which is commonly done to prevent stressed birds attacking each other, is not allowed or necessary; the animals are living in far more natural circumstances, so there is no need for such inhumane practices. Additionally, antibiotics and wormers are only allowed in circumstances where it is absolutely necessary. This means that not only are the animals in better health, but so are the local soils and waterways, as medications are not routinely excreted, and the dairy and eggs do not contain antibiotics that humans then consume.

GROW YOUR OWN

Growing fruit and veg can be very satisfying and is possible even in small spaces.

Consider choosing native varieties which provide food and shelter to wildlife, too. Buying heirloom seeds will help keep a wide variety of food in circulation, and you can save the seeds from your crops to use in subsequent years.

VOTE WITH YOUR MONEY

If you can buy only organic or regeneratively produced food, that is ideal, but in practice it's difficult and expensive. However, even one swap will have a positive impact. Every single purchase is a 'vote with your money', so it is worth choosing food where you know its origin, how it is produced, and whether the producer's ethos aligns with your own beliefs.

The Pesticide Action Network UK (PAN UK) lists the top 12 fruit and vegetables that are most likely to be contaminated with multiple pesticides, which is a great place to start if you are looking to move towards eating more organically but are not sure what to prioritise. Remember: don't stop at food. Cleaning products, clothing, and health and wellness products can also be organic and all have a lower impact.

CHOOSE PLANT-BASED BUTTER AND ALTERNATIVES

All of our recipes will work with a plant-based butter (the type that comes in a block, not in a tub). Dairy products have a huge environmental impact due to the large amount of land the cows need to live on, their high water consumption, and the amount of soya that is grown for their feed. Organic British dairy products are better environmentally than most, and if you have a local organic dairy, you may wish to support them.

Plant-based alternatives can be highly processed, but there are many that are made from simple ingredients, and some that are organic, too. Look for products that are low in highly refined oils and free of artificial additives (if it's hard to pronounce, it's probably an additive!).

SUPPORT CROWDFARMING

Whilst local, organic, regenerative produce is always going to be the best choice, in the UK we are limited by the climate and cannot grow all the food we've been accustomed to eating. CrowdFarming is a wonderful initiative connecting farmers with buyers and cutting out the middleman. From oranges to pomegranates to nuts, you can place an order or sponsor a tree – this is such a lovely way to get quality ingredients whilst being kind to both the farmer and the planet.

SUMMER

Summer feels warmer, slower and lazier than spring, but many fruits burst into life, and in the UK, apricots, blackberries, blackcurrants, blueberries, cherries, gooseberries, plums, raspberries, strawberries and elderflowers are all in season. Choose fruit that is British where possible, and if you find you have too much, make jams, jellies, and preserves so you can have a taste of summer later in the year when the weather turns colder. Our local greengrocer sells fruit cheaply when it's past its best, which is ideal for making jam, so check if yours does too. Just about every cake looks wonderful when piled high with fresh berries, and they can hide a multitude of sins if a bake doesn't quite go to plan. Honey is harvested in summer and goes perfectly with many summer fruits. Choose raw local honey for lower food mileage and antioxidant benefits — many say it even wards off hayfever!

We like to spend as much time as possible outside, enjoying this short season of warmth and long days. We eat outside as much as possible, and it's the perfect time for hosting friends and family and showing off baking skills at picnics and whenever someone pops round. We often cook pancakes over a fire outside, or even bake doughnuts and waffles. Now is the time to reap the benefits if you grow any of your own fruit or veg, and you can forage if not; elderflowers make lovely syrups and drinks, blackberries begin to ripen as summer slows, and in some parts of the country you can even find wild raspberries and strawberries.

APRICOT AND THYME TART

The thyme in this tart adds a fragrant hint of summer, and the plump apricots and almond filling make for a delicious bake. If you'd like to use fresh apricots for this recipe, make the syrup without adding the dried apricots to it. The rest of the recipe will be the same.

Serves: 6-8
Prep time: 50 minutes, plus 30 minutes chilling
Cooking time: 50-55 minutes
Oven temp: 180°C fan

FOR THE PASTRY

185g plain flour

25g caster sugar

115g cold, salted butter, cubed

60ml cold water

1 egg, beaten, to glaze (or 40-50ml milk)

FOR THE SYRUP

100ml water

1 tbsp light soft brown sugar

1 tsp dried thyme

6 dried apricots

1 tbsp apricot jam

FOR THE FRANGIPANE

50g salted butter, softened

1 egg

1 tsp vanilla extract

50g caster sugar

50g ground almonds

10g plain flour

FOR THE TOPPING

½ tbsp flaked almonds

To make the pastry, combine the flour and sugar in a mixing bowl. Add the cubed butter and, using the tips of your fingers, rub the ingredients together until the mixture resembles breadcrumbs.

Gradually add the water and knead until the mixture comes together to form a ball of dough. Wrap the dough in reusable food wrap or pop in an airtight container and refrigerate for 30 minutes. Grease an 8-inch tart tin with butter, then dust with a little flour, shaking out the excess to weigh out for the frangipane.

To make the syrup, combine the water, sugar, thyme and dried apricots in a small pan. Bring to the boil for 2 minutes, then remove the pan from the heat and leave to cool. Once cooled, remove and set aside the now-plump apricots for later. Return the syrup to the heat and bring to a simmer. Reduce until there is about 1 tablespoon of thick syrup, then remove from the heat and stir in the apricot jam. Set aside to cool.

On a floured surface, roll the chilled pastry dough out into a large circle, about 3-4mm thick. Carefully lift the pastry into the prepared tin and gently press the dough into the base, leaving any overhanging dough to allow for shrinkage. If the pastry tears, don't worry, just patch it up with dough.

Prick the base of the pastry with a fork a few times then lay a sheet of baking parchment over the surface. Add a layer of baking beans (or uncooked rice) on top of the paper to weigh down the pastry. Blind bake in the oven for 20 minutes.

Remove the pastry case from the oven and carefully lift off the paper and beans (or rice). Glaze the tart case with beaten egg and bake for 5 minutes to seal the pastry. Carefully cut the overhanging pastry away with a sharp knife then let it cool.

To prepare the frangipane filling, use an electric whisk to beat the butter until creamy. Add the egg and vanilla and mix to combine. Add the sugar, almonds and flour and stir together to form a batter.

Brush the thyme and apricot syrup over the base of the pastry case. Then, using a spatula, spread the frangipane evenly over the top. Arrange the plumped apricots on the surface of the mixture and finish with a sprinkling of flaked almonds.

Bake the tart for 20 to 25 minutes until the pastry is golden and the frangipane filling springs back when gently pressed. Remove from the oven and allow to cool before serving.

RASPBERRY CROISSANTS

The raspberry filling makes a more unusual croissant that is VERY popular with my kids. Though a bit of a long-winded bake, the effort of making croissants is all worthwhile once you take that first bite.

Makes: 6
Prep time: 1 hour 45 minutes, plus 18 hours proving/chilling
Cooking time: 20 minutes
Oven temp: 180°C fan

FOR THE RASPBERRY FILLING

20g dried raspberries

40g ground almonds

20g icing sugar

20g butter

FOR THE CROISSANT DOUGH

300g strong white bread flour

1 tsp salt

30g caster sugar

7g instant yeast

180ml cold water

180g room temperature butter

FOR THE TOPPING

1 egg, beaten, to glaze (or use milk)

10g icing sugar, for dusting

FOR THE RASPBERRY FILLING

Place the dried raspberries in a food processor and blitz until there are no big lumps. Add the ground almonds, icing sugar and butter and blitz together until it forms a soft dough. Using your hands, form into six log shapes, each approximately 10cm long. Place the logs flat on a plate or baking tray and cover with baking parchment, reusable food wrap, or by putting the plate or tray in a bag. Chill in the fridge until ready to use.

FOR THE CROISSANT DOUGH

Add the flour, salt and sugar to a mixing bowl and stir together. Mix the water and yeast in a jug until fully dissolved. Make a well in the middle of the dry ingredients and pour in the yeasty liquid. Stir together until the mixture comes together to form a rough dough.

Place the dough on a floured surface and knead for 10 minutes. Transfer the ball of dough to a lightly oiled bowl, cover with a damp tea towel or clean shower cap, and chill in the fridge for 2 hours.

Meanwhile, put the butter between two sheets of baking parchment and use a rolling pin to bash and roll it – take your time with this step, it is important to break down the butter. Shape the butter into a rectangle, about 20x15cm. Leave it wrapped in the paper and place in the fridge to chill.

Put the ball of chilled dough on a floured work surface and roll it out into a rectangle about 40x20cm. Shape the corners by pulling the dough out with your hands. If the dough shrinks back to an oval, pop it back in the fridge for 10 minutes. Unwrap the slab of butter and place it in the centre of the dough, covering the middle third.

Fold one side of the dough up and halfway over the butter, then fold the other side over the butter in the same way so that the edges of the dough meet and the butter is covered. Fold in half along the line where the dough meets, then wrap in airtight reusable food wrap and return to the fridge for 30 minutes.

Repeat the rolling, folding and chilling process twice more - rolling the dough while it is still folded, without adding more butter. If the butter breaks through the surface of the dough at any point, don't worry, just dust it with a little flour and continue. After the third fold, wrap in reusable food wrap and chill in the fridge overnight. The dough will have 81 layers in total.

FOR THE BAKE

The next day, carefully roll the dough out into a rectangle, about 50x25cm. Neatly trim the edges, then cut the dough into six even triangles, with your knife zig-zagging across the length of the dough.

Taking each triangle in turn, gently pull the two corners at the base to stretch and widen it. Make a small 1cm cut in the centre of the triangle's base – this will help form the crescent shape when it comes to rolling the dough.

Place one of the raspberry fillings just above the small cut you have made, leaving 1cm of dough either side. Starting at the base, gently roll each triangle into a croissant, enclosing the raspberry paste inside. Be careful not to press too hard and crush the delicate layers. Place the rolled croissants on a lined baking tray, making sure the triangles' tips are tucked underneath. Bend the ends of each croissant inwards to create the classic crescent shape. Leave plenty of space between each croissant to allow room to rise, then cover with a damp tea towel and leave to rise for 2 hours, ideally between 18°C and 24°C. Chill in the fridge for 30 minutes before baking.

Generously glaze each croissant with beaten egg, then bake in the centre of the oven for 20 minutes until risen and golden brown. Transfer to a wire rack to cool, then use a sieve to dust the croissants liberally with icing sugar. Serve with coffee and your favourite soft fruits for a truly indulgent breakfast.

BREADCRUMB PLUM CAKE

This sticky, rich cake is popular in Germany and uses stale bread. There really is no need to throw those crusts away! The streusel topping is optional but adds a delicious crunchy texture. It can be baked on top of the cake or separately on a baking tray and added afterwards – just keep an eye on it and ensure it does not burn or it will become bitter.

Serves: 8
Prep time: 55 minutes, plus 1 hour soaking
Cooking time: 45-55 minutes
Oven temp: 180°C fan

FOR THE STREUSEL TOPPING
(OPTIONAL)
60g plain flour
50g demerara sugar
¼ tsp salt
¼ tsp ground cinnamon
40g melted butter, cooled
30g mixed nuts, chopped

FOR THE PLUM TOPPING
4 plums
100ml red wine
80g caster sugar

FOR THE CAKE
100g stale bread, crumbed (any bread will do!)
175g butter, softened
150g light soft brown sugar
2 eggs
70g ground almonds
25g plain flour
1½ tsp baking powder
½ tsp ground cinnamon
1 lemon, zested

Grease and flour an 8-inch cake tin then start by preparing the streusel topping. Mix all the ingredients together and chill in the fridge until ready to bake.

To prepare the plum topping, cut each plum into eighths and warm in a saucepan with the red wine and caster sugar. Simmer gently for 5 minutes then take off the heat and leave to soak for approximately 1 hour.

To make the breadcrumbs, blitz the stale bread in a food processor or tip it into a canvas bag and bashed with a rolling pin – it may help to toast it slightly first depending on how hard it is.

In a large mixing bowl, cream the butter and soft brown sugar together until light and fluffy. Mix in the eggs then add the remaining cake ingredients.

Pour the cake batter into the prepared tin, smoothing it out with a spatula or the back of a spoon. Remove the plums from the syrup with a slotted spoon and arrange them over the top of the cake.

You can choose to crumble the streusel over the top of the cake at this point, or it can be baked separately on a baking tray and added to the cake afterwards (we prefer the latter as it adds a delicious crunch to the soft cake).

Bake the cake for 30 minutes until the top is golden brown and a skewer inserted into the middle comes out clean. If it is not baked, return it to the oven for 5 minutes before checking again. Repeat until cooked. If baking the streusel separately, spread it out evenly on a baking tray and bake with the cake for around 10 minutes. Keep an eye on it as it will burn if left too long.

Whilst the cake is baking, heat the plum syrup to a rolling boil. Boil for around 5 minutes until it has reduced and become a little thicker and stickier.

Once the cake has baked, drizzle the warm syrup over the top. Allow the cake to cool before removing it from the tin. Serve on its own or with a dollop of crème fraîche.

BAKER'S TIP
If you don't have any stale bread, you can use ground almonds instead of breadcrumbs.

DEANNE'S STRAWBERRY CHOUX AU CRAQUELIN

Deanne, our product developer at Honeywell Bakes, says: "I love French pastries, so I had to conquer the choux au craquelin as they are so delicious and look amazing. This recipe was included as one of Honeywell's subscription bakes and they can be styled with any seasonal fruit."

Makes: 9
Prep time: 40 minutes
Cooking time: 2 hours 20 minutes
Oven temp: 200°C fan

FOR THE CRÈME PÂTISSIÈRE

3 egg yolks

50g light soft brown sugar

15g cornflour

150g milk

½ tsp vanilla extract

10g butter, softened

60ml double cream

FOR THE CRAQUELIN

50g plain flour

50g golden caster sugar

A few drops of red food colouring

40g cold butter, cubed

FOR THE STRAWBERRY COMPOTE

50g strawberries

25g caster sugar

½ tsp vanilla extract

FOR THE CHOUX PASTRY

60ml milk

50g unsalted butter

60ml water

75g plain flour

2 eggs, beaten

YOU WILL NEED:

Download ours, or draw a template with 6cm circles, 4cm apart (to ensure your choux buns are the same size and evenly spaced)

2 x piping bags with a 1cm tip

A circular cutter, 5cm in diameter, for the craquelin

FOR THE CRÈME PÂTISSIÈRE

Place the egg yolks, brown sugar and cornflour in a large bowl and whisk together. Mix the milk and vanilla extract together in a small pan then warm over a medium heat until it starts to bubble gently at the sides. Remove from the heat and pour half of the warm milk into the bowl of egg yolk mixture, whisking briskly for about 30 seconds. Return the egg mixture to the pan with the remaining milk and cook over a medium heat, whisking constantly, until very thick.

Remove from the heat and stir in the butter until fully combined. Leave to stand for 10 minutes, whisking every so often, then transfer to a bowl and leave to cool for 5 minutes. Place a piece of cling film directly onto the surface of the mixture to prevent a skin forming, then refrigerate until ready to fill the choux buns (at which point you will add the double cream).

FOR THE CRAQUELIN

Combine the flour, golden caster sugar and food colouring in a bowl. Add the butter and rub the ingredients together between your fingertips until it resembles breadcrumbs, then knead together to form a dough. Place the dough between two sheets of baking parchment and roll out to approximately 2-3mm thick, then transfer to a baking tray and place in the freezer until later.

FOR THE STRAWBERRY COMPOTE

Place the strawberries, caster sugar and vanilla extract in a small saucepan over a low heat for 10 to 15 minutes, stirring regularly until you have a thick, sticky compote. Transfer to a small bowl and leave to cool until you are ready to fill the buns.

FOR THE CHOUX PASTRY

Line a baking tray with baking parchment and position your template underneath the paper. Add the milk, butter and water to a saucepan and gently heat. Once the butter has just melted, increase the heat until the liquid comes to a fast boil. Immediately turn off the heat, then add the flour and beat vigorously with a wooden spoon until you have a smooth dough that comes away from the sides of the pan. Allow to cool for 10 minutes.

Gradually add the beaten eggs a little at a time, mixing well with a wooden spoon or electric hand mixer. At first, the mixture might separate, but keep mixing and the dough will come together. It is ready when it reaches a glossy, pipeable consistency and the mixture reluctantly drops off the spoon in a V shape. Be careful to add the beaten egg slowly – you may not need it all and if you add too much you cannot add more flour at this stage! Spoon the mixture into a piping bag with a 1cm tip then, using the template as a guide, pipe nine rounds onto the prepared tray in a continuous motion. Wet a finger with water and dab the tops to flatten any peaks.

TO ASSEMBLE THE CHOUX AU CRAQUELIN

Remove the sheet of craquelin from the freezer and, using a cookie cutter, carefully cut out nine thin discs. Work as quickly as possible to prevent the discs from softening. Use a spatula to gently lift the discs and place one on top of each choux bun. Bake the buns in the oven for 40 minutes.

Remove the golden, puffed-up choux buns from the oven and leave to cool. Once cooled carefully cut the top off each bun using a sharp knife.

To finish the filling, beat the double cream until soft peaks form, then fold it through the crème pâtissière. Spoon the mixture into a piping bag, tie a knot in the opening, and set it aside. Spoon the strawberry compote into a second piping bag with a 1cm tip.

Pipe crème pâtissière into each choux bun, then pipe some compote before replacing the 'lid'. Top each bun with a slice of fresh strawberry, if you wish. Choux au craquelin are best served fresh but will keep in an airtight container in the fridge for 2 days, although the pasty will be less crisp.

Scan for template

CHOCOLATE STALE BREAD CAKE

Once you try this cake, you will not waste bread again! It is a rich, creamy cake that pairs wonderfully with fresh fruit and a generous scoop of good quality vanilla ice cream.

Serves: 6
Prep time: 50 minutes
Cooking time: 45 minutes
Oven temp: 170°C fan

250g stale bread
500ml milk
2 eggs
150g granulated sugar
80g vegetable oil
1 tbsp plain flour
2 tsp baking powder
70g cocoa powder
A pinch of salt
200g chocolate chips
60g raisins (optional)
50g nuts, chopped (optional)

Grease an 8-inch cake tin and dust the base and sides with cocoa powder.

Soak the bread in the milk for 20 to 30 minutes until the milk has been absorbed and the bread is soft. Mix together until creamy (particularly hard bread may take a little longer).

In a separate bowl, beat the sugar and eggs together until light and foamy. Slowly add the oil, beating as you do, then beat together for 1 minute.

Sift in the flour, baking powder, and cocoa powder, then mix until well combined.

Add the chocolate chips, bread mixture, and raisins and nuts (if using), then mix thoroughly before pouring the batter into the prepared tin.

Bake for 40 to 45 minutes until nicely risen and a skewer inserted in the centre comes out clean.

Leave to cool in the tin for 30 minutes before transferring to a wire rack to cool completely. To serve, pile high with the fruit of your choice and dust with icing sugar before slicing.

COURGETTE CAKE

This tea-loaf style cake makes good use of courgettes and is very adaptable – try changing the nuts and spices according to what you have to hand. The courgettes make it deliciously moist, and we recommend trying it warm with melty butter. Yum!

Makes: 1 loaf
Prep time: 35 minutes
Cooking time: 50 minutes
Oven temp: 160°C fan

2 eggs
125ml vegetable oil
85g light soft brown sugar
350g courgette, grated
1 orange, zested and juiced
1 tsp vanilla extract
300g plain flour
2 tsp ground cinnamon
½ tsp ground nutmeg
1 tsp mixed spice
½ tsp bicarbonate of soda
½ tsp baking powder
85g pecans, roughly chopped
120g raisins
50g prunes or dates, chopped
A pinch of salt
2 tbsp demerara sugar, for topping

Butter a 2lb loaf tin and dust the base and sides thoroughly with flour.

In a large bowl, whisk together the eggs, oil and sugar. Squeeze the grated courgettes to remove any excess moisture, then add them to the bowl along with the orange zest and juice and vanilla.

In a separate bowl, mix together the dry ingredients (excluding the demerara sugar) and the chopped fruit and nuts until well combined. Add the wet and dry mixtures together and stir well before pouring into the prepared tin. Sprinkle the demerara sugar over the top.

Bake for 50 minutes – it's ready when a skewer inserted into the centre comes out clean.

LUCY'S PAVLOVA

Lucy Prigmore, Biscuit Bakery Manager at Honeywell Bakes, says: "My pavlova is always requested at family parties as it's a firm favourite. I love this recipe as it's gluten-free and tastes and looks fantastic!"

Serves: 8
Prep time: 30 minutes
Cooking time: 1 hour 15 minutes
Oven temp: 110°C fan

FOR THE MERINGUE

6 egg whites

¼ tsp white wine vinegar

350g caster sugar

1 tsp cornflour

FOR THE TOPPING

350g double cream

1 tbsp icing sugar, plus extra to dust

250g berries or fruit (this recipe is very adaptable, so choose your favourites)

Draw a circle, approximately 10 inches in diameter, on a piece of baking parchment (cake or pastry tins can be helpful templates). Place the paper upside down on a baking tray so the circle is facing down but still visible through the paper.

In a clean bowl, use an electric whisk to beat the egg whites and vinegar until they form soft peaks. Combine the caster sugar and cornflour in a separate bowl and add it to the egg white a little at a time whilst whisking continuously. Repeat until all the sugar and cornflour has been whisked in, and until you can no longer feel the sugar crystals when you rub a small amount of the mixture between your thumb and forefinger.

Pile the meringue onto the prepared baking parchment in a dome shape, using the circle as a guide. Flatten the top then use the back of a metal spoon to drag up the sides and create the effect overleaf. Bake for 1 hour and 15 minutes before turning the oven off. Leave the meringue in the oven overnight or until completely cool and set.

When ready to decorate, whisk the double cream until stiff, then mix in a tablespoon of icing sugar. Add the cream to the top of the meringue, then scatter with fruit and berries of your choosing. Dust with icing sugar to finish.

LUCY'S TIP

This pavlova works well in any season. Try piling it high with cranberries, blueberries and orange segments in winter, or with figs, blackberries and pear slices in autumn.

GINGER AND APRICOT CREAMS

A delicious addition to any summer picnic, these biscuits also go perfectly with a cup of tea. They have just the right amount of sweetness.

Makes: 8
Prep time: 45 minutes, plus 15 minutes chilling
Cooking time: 12 minutes
Oven temp: 160°C fan

FOR THE BISCUITS

110g plain flour

85g demerara sugar

1 ½ tsp ground ginger

½ tsp bicarbonate of soda

50g cold butter, cubed

35g dried apricots, finely chopped

25g beaten egg

½ tbsp milk

FOR THE FILLING

30g white chocolate

35g butter, softened

35g full-fat soft cheese

70g icing sugar

FOR THE TOPPING

20g white chocolate

1 tbsp crystallised ginger, finely chopped (optional)

YOU WILL NEED

Piping bag with a 1cm tip (or you can use a spoon)

In a bowl, combine the flour, demerara sugar, ginger, and bicarbonate of soda. Add the cold butter and, using your fingertips, rub it into the flour until the mixture resembles breadcrumbs. Add the finely chopped apricots and stir evenly through the mixture.

In a separate bowl, beat together the egg and milk, then slowly add it to the flour-butter mixture, bringing it together to form a dough. Wrap the dough in reusable food wrap and place in the fridge to chill for 15 minutes.

Line two baking trays with silicone sheets or baking parchment and set aside. Then, roll tablespoon-sized scoops of dough into balls and place eight on each prepared tray, leaving even spaces in between. Bake in the centre of the oven for approximately 12 minutes or until golden.

Remove the baked biscuits from the oven and transfer to a wire rack to cool completely.

Whilst waiting for the biscuits to cool, prepare the filling. Melt the white chocolate in a microwaveable bowl in 30-second bursts until melted. Beat the softened butter until light and fluffy, then fold in the melted white chocolate beforing mixing in the soft cheese until just combined. Sift in the icing sugar and quickly mix together. Be careful not to overmix the filling or it will become too runny. Chill in the fridge until ready to fill the biscuits.

When ready, spoon the filling into a piping bag with a 1cm tip. Pipe a generous amount onto the underside of one of the biscuits, then sandwich another on top. Repeat with the remaining biscuits until they've all been filled.

Melt the white chocolate as before and drizzle over the biscuits, then finish with a sprinkling of chopped crystallised ginger.

PERSIAN LOVE CAKE

Legend has it there was once a woman who fell deeply in love with a Persian prince, and she created this cake in a bid to win his heart. Even if you don't succeed in charming a royal with your beautiful bake, at least you'll have a delicious cake to devour!

Serves: 6
Prep time: 1 hour
Cooking time: 30 minutes
Oven temp: 140°C fan

FOR THE CAKE

65g salted butter

50g caster sugar

1 egg

¼ tsp ground cardamom

60g self-raising flour

65g ground almonds

1 tsp milk

½ lemon, zested and juiced

FOR THE DRIZZLE

2 tsp caster sugar

½ lemon, juiced

5ml rose water

FOR THE ICING

50g icing sugar

¼ lemon, juiced

½ tsp cold water

FOR THE DECORATION

1 tbsp rose petals

1 tbsp pistachios, chopped

Grease a 6-inch cake tin then lightly dust the base and sides with flour.

Place the butter and sugar in a mixing bowl and cream together with a wooden spoon, then beat in the egg until smooth. Add the ground cardamom, flour, ground almonds, milk, and lemon zest and juice to the mixture and stir together until well combined.

Spoon the cake batter into the prepared tin and bake for 20 minutes. Check if the cake is ready by poking the centre with a cocktail stick – if it comes out clean and dry, it's baked; if not, return to the oven for 5 minutes then check again.

Remove the cake from the oven and set aside whilst you make the drizzle syrup. Add the sugar, lemon juice and rose water to a small saucepan and warm over a low heat until the sugar dissolves.

Carefully remove the warm cake from the tin and transfer to a wire rack. Using a cocktail stick, poke holes all over the surface of the cake, being careful not to go all the way through to the bottom. Drizzle the warm syrup over the top and leave to cool completely.

Once the cake has cooled, make the icing in a small bowl by combining the icing sugar, lemon juice and cold water until a smooth, thick consistency.

Spoon the icing over the cake, allowing it to drip down the sides. Finish with a sprinkling of rose petals and chopped pistachios. The cake will keep for a few days in an airtight container when stored at room temperature.

BAKER'S TIP

You can dry your own rose petals by spreading them in a warm dry place for a day or two. Just be sure that they are chemical-free and picked on a dry day.

SUMMER FRUIT LAYER CAKE

You can use any fruit to make this cake, and with fresh, colourful berries on top, it makes a real showstopper.

Serves: 20
Prep time: 45 minutes
Cooking time: 45 minutes
Oven temp: 160°C fan

FOR THE CAKE

450g salted butter

450g golden caster sugar

525g self-raising flour

9 eggs

2 tsp vanilla extract

600g summer berries

FOR THE BUTTERCREAM

300g salted butter, softened

600g icing sugar

1 tsp vanilla extract

TO DECORATE

Summer fruits, such as strawberries, blackberries, raspberries, blueberries, and red or blackcurrants

Grease three 8-inch cake tins and lightly dust the base and sides with plain flour. In a large mixing bowl, use an electric whisk to cream the butter and sugar until light and fluffy. Add the flour, eggs and vanilla extract and mix until well combined, then fold in the fruit.

Split the mixture evenly between the three tins and bake the cakes for around 40 minutes. If necessary, carefully move them around after 30 minutes so they bake evenly. Once baked, a skewer inserted into the centre should come out clean (though it may take a little longer due to the moisture from the fruit).

Remove from the oven and leave to cool in the tin for 15 to 20 minutes before transferring to a wire rack. Allow to cool fully before decorating.

To make the buttercream, beat the butter for a few minutes with an electric whisk until pale and soft. Add the icing sugar and vanilla extract and beat until smooth.

To decorate, place one cake onto a cake stand or serving platter and spread about a quarter of the buttercream on top. Place the next cake on top and repeat, then finish with the third cake. Use the remaining buttercream to cover the top and sides. It's okay to have a thin layer and some cake showing through – a rustic look is what you are going for! Just before serving, pile the summer fruits on top and around the base, if desired.

EDWARD'S CHOCOLATE FRENCH TOAST

This is my son Edward's favourite brunch at any time of year. A sweet and indulgent treat, it's always quickly devoured by hungry children. It's perfect for using up stale bread, and you can use any bread you have - from brioche to baguettes, anything goes!

Serves 4
Prep time: 10 minutes
Cooking time: 15 minutes

2 eggs

250g milk

2 tbsp sugar (we love using golden caster sugar, but any sugar will do)

2 tsp vanilla extract

8 slices of bread (or more if using sliced baguette)

6 tbsp chocolate spread

Butter, for frying

TO SERVE

Icing sugar, for dusting

Berries or other fruit

Whisk the eggs, milk, sugar and vanilla extract together in a shallow bowl.

Make chocolate spread sandwiches and cut each one into three fingers (unless using sliced baguette or a narrower bread).

Heat a knob of butter in a frying pan until bubbling, then dip each sandwich into the whisked egg mixture and leave to soak for about 30 seconds.

Fill the frying pan with the egg-soaked sandwiches and fry for a few minutes on each side until golden brown. Repeat until you've fried all of the French toast.

Serve with a dusting of icing sugar and some fresh fruit.

BAKER'S TIP

If you make too much, you can save the spare French toast and reheat it in a frying pan when you next fancy it. It will keep wrapped in the fridge for a day or two.

JILL'S GINGER BISCUITS

I met Jill when I lived in Yorkshire and we became instant friends. She was often baking and this is one of her favourite recipes. These biscuits are a great, simple, traditional, an old-fashioned bake from her Aunt Nelly, which we've converted from ounces for you.

Makes: 12
Prep time: 10 minutes
Cooking time: 15 minutes
Oven temp: 155°C fan

115g butter
1 tbsp golden syrup
170g self-raising flour
85g sugar
1 heaped tsp ground ginger
A pinch of bicarbonate of soda

Gently melt the butter and syrup together in a heavy-bottomed pan.

Mix the remaining dry ingredients in a bowl, then add the warm syrup and butter and combine until it forms a dough.

Roll into balls, about a teaspoon of mixture each, and place on a baking tray lined with a reusable silicone sheet or baking parchment. Allow space between each biscuit so they can spread as they cook.

Bake in the oven for about 10 minutes until golden. Transfer to a wire rack to cool before enjoying with a cup of tea.

JILL'S TIP

The dough should only be a little sticky – if it's too wet, it will spread too much in the oven.

Add some chopped crystallised ginger for an extra fiery kick. The recipe doubles easily.

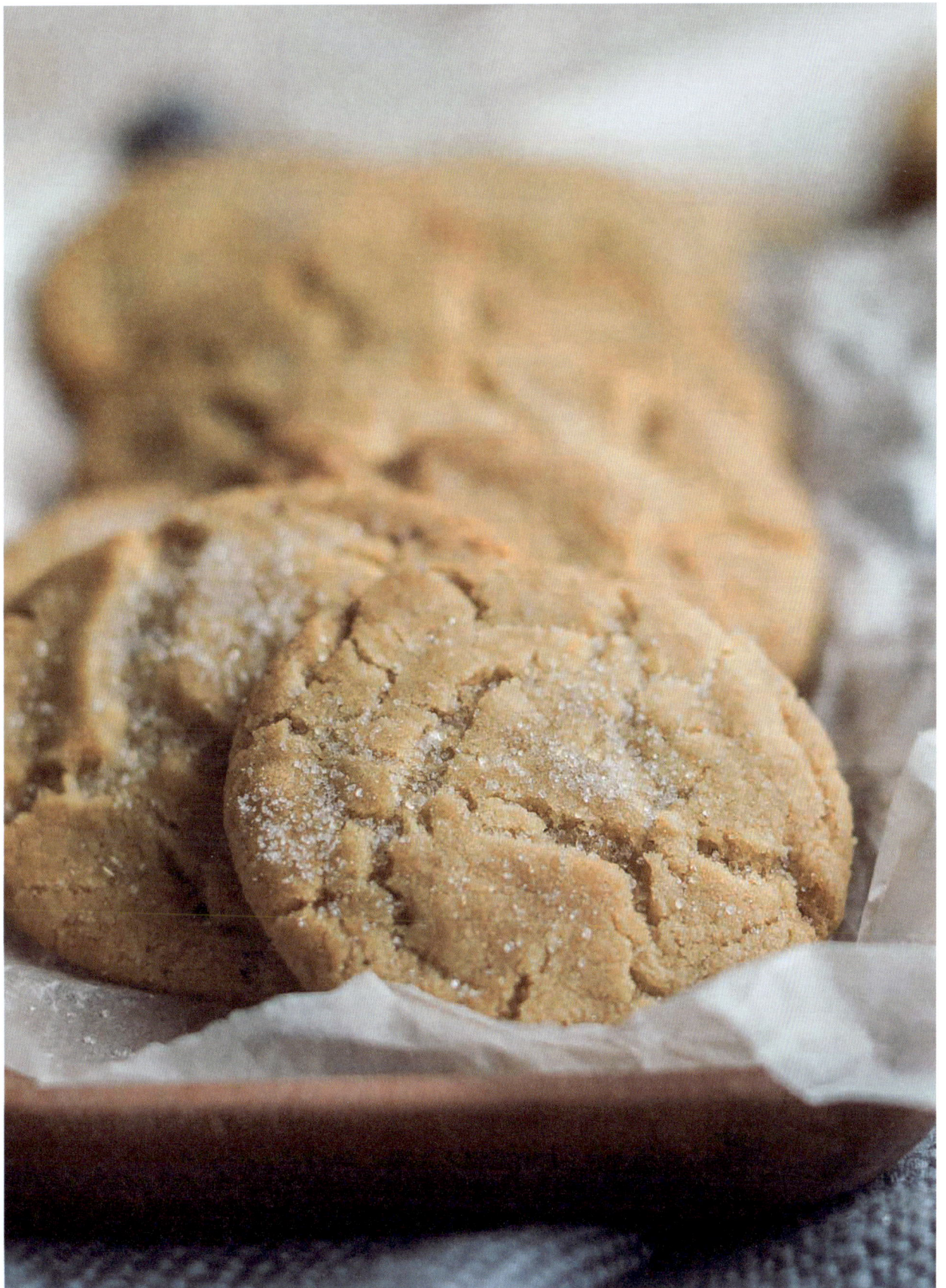

SIM'S RASPBERRY AND WHITE CHOCOLATE CUPCAKES

Sim, my sister-in-law, says: "These white chocolate and raspberry cupcakes are a real favourite of mine, especially when the garden is bursting with fresh raspberries. The sweetness of the white chocolate with the tang of the raspberries is such a perfect match, and the soft, buttery sponge makes them so hard to resist. I love making them for family or friends, whether it's a summer get-together or just because. If you've got fresh raspberries, these are a must-bake – trust me, they never last long!"

Makes: 12
Prep time: 45 minutes
Cooking time: 18-20 minutes
Oven temp: 180°C fan

FOR THE CUPCAKES

170g butter, softened

170g caster sugar

3 eggs

170g self-raising flour

120g raspberries

120g white chocolate chips

FOR THE ICING

225g white chocolate chips

275g butter, softened

1 tsp vanilla extract

275g icing sugar

12 raspberries

YOU WILL NEED

12 cupcake cases

Piping bag

In a large bowl, using a handheld electric whisk (or a standard whisk and elbow grease!), whisk together the butter and sugar until pale and fluffy. Add the eggs and mix well, then fold in the flour until well combined. Fold in the raspberries and white chocolate chips.

Put the cupcake cases in a cupcake tin then divide the mixture evenly between the cases.

Bake for 18 to 20 minutes until risen, slightly golden, and a skewer inserted into the centre of a cupcake comes out clean. Allow to cool completely.

To make the icing, melt the white chocolate chips in a bowl over a pan of simmering water, then set aside to cool but not set. In a separate bowl, beat the butter with an electric whisk until pale and creamy. Add the cooled white chocolate and vanilla extract and whisk together.

Sift in the icing sugar and mix well, then whisk for a few minutes until light and fluffy. Add to a piping bag fitted with a medium tip, or cut off about 1 cm from the end. Pipe whirls onto the top of each cupcake and finish with a fresh raspberry.

BAKER'S TIP

You can use dried or frozen raspberries in this recipe, but fresh raspberries look great on the top of each cupcake. If using frozen raspberries, use them as soon as they are taken out of the freezer so they don't go soft and mushy.

LIME AND COCONUT CAKE

An easy cake that is zesty and unique. A great alternative to a lemon drizzle.

Makes: 1 loaf
Prep time: 40 minutes
Cooking time: 50 minutes
Oven temp: 160°C fan

FOR THE CAKE

150g butter, softened

150g caster sugar

2 eggs

2 tbsp milk

150g self-raising flour

1 lime, zested

FOR THE SYRUP

2 tsp caster sugar

1 lime, juiced

½ tsp water

FOR THE ICING

50g icing sugar

25g white chocolate

FOR THE TOPPING

Desiccated coconut

Lime zest

Grease a 2lb loaf tin and dust the base and sides with flour.

In a mixing bowl, cream together the butter and caster sugar until light and fluffy, then gradually beat in the eggs and milk. Sift in the flour and mix until smooth, then fold in the lime zest.

Pour the batter into the loaf tin and smooth the surface with the back of a spoon, then bake for 40 to 45 minutes. Test the cake by poking a skewer into the centre: if it comes out clean, the cake is baked; if not, return to the oven for a further 5 minutes and test again.

Remove from the oven and set aside whilst you make the syrup. Stir the sugar, lime juice and water in a small saucepan over a low heat until the sugar dissolves.

Carefully remove the warm cake from the tin and place on a wire rack. Using a cocktail stick, poke holes all over the surface of the cake, being careful not to go all the way through to the bottom. Drizzle over the lime syrup and leave to cool completely.

To prepare the icing, add the icing sugar to a bowl. Melt the white chocolate in the microwave or over a bain-marie, then add it to the bowl and mix to form a thick icing. Using a spoon, swirl the icing on top of the cake before finishing with a sprinkling of desiccated coconut and lime zest. Enjoy!

LEMON AND BLUEBERRY PULL-APART BREAD

When we test-baked this in the bakery, several members of the team voted it as the most delicious bread ever. It's best when warm with a cup of coffee or tea. Share with friends on a summer's day!

Makes: 1 loaf
Prep time: 1 hour, plus 1 hour 30 minutes proving
Cooking time: 25-30 minutes
Oven temp: 180°C fan

FOR THE DOUGH

255g plain flour

40g caster sugar

½ tsp salt

60l milk

45g butter

45ml water

1 ½ tsp instant yeast

1 ½ tsp vanilla extract

1 egg

FOR THE FILLING

75g granulated sugar

1 lemon, zested

25g butter, melted

3 tbsp dried blueberries or 100g fresh (30g whole; 70g chopped)

In a large bowl, or the bowl of a stand mixer with the dough hook attached, combine the flour, sugar and salt.

Add the milk, butter and water to a small saucepan and stir on a low heat until the butter melts and the mixture is warm, but not hot, to the touch. Add the yeast and mix together. Set aside for a few minutes then add the yeast liquid, vanilla extract and egg to the dry ingredients.

Mix to form a dough, then knead for 10 to 15 minutes until the dough is smooth and elastic. Cover the bowl with a clean shower cap or a clean, damp tea towel and leave in a warm place to rise for 1 hour or until doubled in size.

Whilst the dough rises, prepare the filling. Combine the granulated sugar and lemon zest and set aside to infuse. Grease and line a 2lb loaf tin, then just before the dough is ready to shape, melt the butter.

Once risen, divide the dough into 12 even portions. Lightly dust the work surface with flour and roughly roll the dough into balls and flatten into discs – they don't need to be perfect circles.

Generously brush each piece of dough with the melted butter then sprinkle over the lemony sugar. Evenly scatter two thirds of the blueberries onto the dough. If using dried blueberries, place the remaining two thirds in a cup and cover with 1 tablespoon of cold water. Leave to rehydrate until later.

Fold each dough circle in half, enclosing the filling inside like a small taco. Arrange the folded portions of dough in the prepared tin, standing upright along the folded edges and lined up in a row. Loosely cover the tin with a clean, damp tea towel and leave to rise for about 30 minutes or until doubled in size.

Once risen, arrange the remaining blueberries on the surface of the bread, tucking them between the layers a little. Put the loaf tin on a baking tray and place it in the centre of the oven for 25 to 30 minutes until it is golden brown and its base sounds hollow when tapped. If the loaf looks like it is at risk of over-browning, cover it loosely with aluminium foil or put a roasting tin on the oven shelf above to bake it more evenly and allow some room for rising.

Remove the baked bread from the oven and leave to cool in the tin for about 15 minutes. The bread is best served whilst still warm.

CHERRY AND ALMOND VIENNESE WHIRLS

These melt-in-the-mouth biscuits are like little bites of summer and are absolute heaven with a cup of tea. If you have fresh or frozen cherries, you can use them instead of dried cherries for the curd, and the flavour will be a bit softer. Not got any cherries? You can use any other curd or jam, and these will still be delicious.

Makes: 12
Prep time: 1 hour, plus 30 minutes chilling
Cooking time: 35 minutes
Oven temp: 160°C fan

FOR THE CHERRY CURD

30g dried cherries (or 120g fresh or frozen cherries)

3 tbsp hot water

50g salted butter

100g caster sugar

2 egg yolks

FOR THE BISCUIT DOUGH

150g plain flour

100g almond flour

50g icing sugar

50g cornflour

250g salted butter, softened

½ tsp vanilla extract

1 tsp milk

FOR THE BUTTERCREAM

100g salted butter, softened

220g icing sugar

2 tsp vanilla extract

2 tsp milk

YOU WILL NEED

A piping bag

A star tip for the piping bag (optional, these can be done without, but the biscuits won't have the traditional pattern)

To make the cherry curd, begin by adding the dried cherries to a small bowl with 3 tablespoons of hot water. Leave for 5 minutes to rehydrate. If using fresh or frozen cherries, you can skip this step.

Place a heatproof bowl over a pan of simmering water, making sure the bowl doesn't touch the surface of the water. Heat together the butter, sugar, and cherries (along with any liquid from the cherries) until the butter has melted. Slowly add the egg yolks, stirring continuously. Continue to cook the curd for 10 minutes or until it's the consistency of custard.

Pass the curd through a sieve, discarding the remaining cherries, and set aside for later use.

To make the biscuit dough, combine the plain flour, almond flour, icing sugar and cornflour in a mixing bowl. Add the softened butter, vanilla extract, and milk, mixing all the ingredients together until a soft dough forms.

If necessary, snip about 1cm off the tip of a piping bag and position the star nozzle in the hole. Spoon the dough into the bag and tie a knot in the opening.

Evenly pipe 24 Viennese whirl biscuits onto two baking parchment-lined baking trays. Start piping from the outside, finishing the swirl in the centre. It may be helpful to print or draw a template of 12 circles, 6cm in diameter, spaced evenly on an A4 sheet. Place this under the baking parchment and use the circles as a guide, but don't forget to remove the paper carefully before baking!

Place the tray of biscuits in the fridge to chill for 30 minutes. Clean the piping bag and nozzle in hot soapy water before drying thoroughly (you will need them for the buttercream).

After chilling, bake the biscuits for 12 to 15 minutes, or until golden around the edges, then allow them to cool.

To prepare the buttercream filling, place the butter in a mixing bowl and beat until creamy. Add the icing sugar, vanilla extract, and milk, continuing to mix until very light and fluffy. Position the clean star nozzle in the piping bag as before and spoon the buttercream into the bag.

Once cooled, carefully pipe the buttercream onto the underside of 12 of the biscuits, but be gentle as they're quite fragile! Spread the cherry curd onto the remaining 12 biscuits, then gently sandwich the two halves together to complete the Viennese whirls. Serve with a hot cup of your favourite tea and enjoy!

LEMON DAISY BISCUITS

This is a classic biscuit recipe with the addition of lemon, and it makes for a delicious bit of summer when sandwiched with citrus icing. Have fun piping the biscuits and practising your royal icing skills!

Makes: 12
Prep time: 1 hour, plus 30 minutes chilling
Cooking time: 10-12 minutes
Oven temp: 160°C fan

FOR THE LEMON BISCUIT

170g butter, softened

100g caster sugar

1 egg, beaten

1 lemon, zested

310g plain flour

½ tsp baking powder

FOR THE LEMON FILLING

80g butter, softened

160g icing sugar

2 tbsp lemon juice

FOR THE ROYAL ICING

200g icing sugar

1 egg white

Water (as needed)

Yellow sprinkles, to decorate (optional)

YOU WILL NEED

A 6cm flower cookie cutter (or paper template, or other shape cutter)

A piping bag or bottle with a 1cm tip

A piping bag or bottle with a 3mm tip

To make the biscuits, beat the butter and caster sugar in a mixing bowl using a wooden spoon or electric handheld mixer until creamy. Add the beaten egg and lemon zest and combine, then sift in the flour and baking powder and mix until it forms a ball of dough. Using a rolling pin, roll out the dough on a lightly floured surface to an even thickness of approximately 5mm.

Use a cookie cutter or template to cut out 24 biscuits, re-rolling any leftover dough as needed. Line a baking tray with baking parchment or a silicone sheet and place your biscuits on the tray, making sure to leave a 2cm gap between each biscuit. Refrigerate for 30 minutes to chill and prevent the biscuits from spreading during baking.

Once chilled, put the baking tray of biscuits in the oven and bake for 10 to 12 minutes or until golden around the edges, turning the tray halfway through to make sure they bake evenly. Remove them from the oven and let them cool completely.

Meanwhile, make the lemon filling. Beat the butter in a bowl with a wooden spoon or electric mixer until soft and creamy. Slowly add the icing sugar, mixing together until fluffy. Add the lemon juice and stir everything together to combine.

Spoon the filling into a piping bag or bottle with a 1cm tip (see Baker's Tip). Pipe some filling onto the underside of one of the cooled biscuits then sandwich another biscuit on top. Repeat with the remaining biscuits.

Once all of the biscuits have been sandwiched together, it's time to decorate! Sift the icing sugar into a bowl and add the egg white. Beat together until smooth and white. The icing should be the consistency of toothpaste. If it's too stiff, add a drop or two of water; if it's too runny, add a little more icing sugar. Spoon the icing into a piping bag or bottle with a 3mm tip.

Scatter the sprinkles, if using, onto a plate. Pipe a blob of icing onto the centre of each sandwiched biscuit, then turn the biscuit upside down and dip it into the sprinkles. Repeat with the remaining biscuit sandwiches.

Use the remaining white icing to pipe petals onto each biscuit, trying different designs if you like. Set aside for 30 minutes to let the icing harden, then enjoy with your favourite drink!

BAKER'S TIP

Stand the piping bag in a mug to fill it more easily. If you don't have a piping tip, snip a small piece off the end of the bag to make a hole approximately 1cm in diameter.

The main issue people encounter when making royal icing is making it too runny. You need it to be thick enough to hold its shape. It's better to be too thick than too thin!

Scan for template

BAKED FRUIT CHEESECAKE

A rich, decadent baked cheesecake that is a real showstopper. When you bring this out at the BBQ, you will hear lots of excited gasps!

Serves: 10
Prep time: 45 minutes, plus 2-12 hours chilling
Cook time: 1 hour 35 minutes
Oven temp: 150°C fan

FOR THE CHEESECAKE

400g ginger biscuits

200g butter, melted

900g full-fat soft cheese

300g buttermilk (or slightly sour milk)

200g icing sugar

2 eggs

2 egg yolks

2 tsp vanilla extract

FOR THE FRUIT

600g stone fruits, such as plums, peaches, apricots or nectarines (approx.)

100g blackberries or raspberries (approx.)

2 tbsp honey or maple syrup

4 tbsp dessert wine (optional)

1 tsp vanilla extract

FOR THE CHEESECAKE

Thoroughly grease a 9-inch springform tin, then blitz the biscuits to a crumb using a food processor or put them in a bag and bash them with a rolling pin. When fully crushed, mix the biscuit crumbs and melted butter together in a bowl. Press the biscuit mixture firmly into the base of the tin, using the back of a spoon to form an even layer.

To make the cheesecake filling, whisk together the soft cheese, buttermilk, sugar, eggs, egg yolks, and vanilla in a jug or bowl. When combined, pour the mixture over the biscuit base before transferring to the oven. Bake for 30 minutes before turning the oven down to 130°C fan and baking for a further 40 minutes. When the cheesecake appears firm and has a slight ripple on the surface when moved, turn the oven off and leave the cheesecake to cool in the oven.

When completely cooled, chill the cheesecake in the fridge for a minimum of 2 hours but preferably overnight.

FOR THE FRUIT

Remove the stones from the stone fruit and cut them into halves, quarters or eighths depending on their size. Toss them in a roasting tin with the honey, wine and vanilla and cook for 15 to 20 minutes at 160°C fan until the fruit starts to soften but still holds its shape. Add the berries to the tin and gently spoon some liquid over them, then cook for 3 to 4 minutes until they look shiny and plump. Remove from the oven and allow to cool. When you are ready to serve the cheesecake, pile the fruit on top, allowing some of the juice to drip down the sides if you wish.

BAKER'S TIP

If there is too much fruit, you can also serve it alongside the cheesecake or pop it in the fridge to enjoy on porridge, yoghurt or granola for a delicious treat at breakfast.

LAURA'S FRUIT SHORTBREAD

Laura is the oldest of my younger sisters, and we have been inseparable since day one! She says: "This adaptable shortbread can be made using whatever berries or fruit you have to hand. We used blackcurrants as they grow in the garden and the tartness complements the sweet shortbread beautifully. It's the most moreish thing I have ever eaten, and I could quite easily devour an entire tray! I always make it with fruit I have grown or foraged; I keep blackcurrants and rhubarb in the freezer specifically for a taste of sunshine in winter."

Makes: 12 slices
Prep time: 30 minutes
Cooking time: 30 minutes
Oven temp: 170°C fan

FOR THE SHORTBREAD

450g plain flour

300g salted butter, cubed

150g caster sugar

1 orange, zested

FOR THE FILLING

300g blackcurrants, or other berries or currants (gooseberries work well)

20g demerara sugar (adjust to taste)

1 tbsp orange juice

Line a 20x25cm baking tin with baking parchment – the paper needs to come up the sides or the filling may stick.

Add the flour and butter into a bowl then use your fingers to rub them together until the mixture resembles fine breadcrumbs. Stir in the sugar and orange zest.

Transfer two thirds of the mixture into the prepared tin and press it down so it covers the base evenly. Prick several times with a fork then bake for 15 minutes until lightly golden.

Whilst the shortbread bakes, prepare the filling. Add the blackcurrants, demerara sugar and orange juice to a saucepan. Heat over a medium heat until the berries have cooked down and the juices have been released. Simmer gently for about 10 minutes to reduce slightly, then allow to cool.

Remove the shortbread from the oven and spread the fruit filling over the top. Use your fingers to spread the remaining shortbread over the top – it will be patchy, but that is okay.

Return to the oven for about 15 minutes until the shortbread topping is golden. Remove and allow to cool in the tin for 30 minutes. Lift the shortbread out of the tin using the baking parchment and allow it to cool fully before cutting into 12 slices.

LAURA'S TIP

For a festive twist, try filling with mincemeat instead of fruit.

SUMMER FRUIT DRIZZLE

This cake can use any fruit you have to hand, and it's a very quick and easy bake that can be whipped up when you don't have a lot of time.

Makes: 1 loaf
Prep time: 30 minutes
Cooking time: 1 hour
Oven temp: 160°C fan

175g butter, softened

175g caster sugar

250g self-raising flour

2 eggs

2 tsp vanilla extract

200g fruit, chopped into 2cm pieces (use whichever summer fruit you wish, but if using stoned fruit, remove the stones before weighing)

140g granulated sugar

1-2 tbsp citrus juice

Grease a 2lb loaf tin and thoroughly dust the base and sides with flour.

Using an electric hand mixer (or a wooden spoon and elbow grease!), beat the butter and caster sugar together in a large mixing bowl until pale and creamy. Add the flour, eggs and vanilla extract and mix until well combined. This mixture will be thicker than a standard sponge.

Spread about one third of the mixture into the loaf tin, then scatter over about 30g of fruit. Add another third of the mixture then another 30g or so of fruit before topping with the remaining mixture and carefully spreading it out with a spatula or the back of a spoon.

Bake the cake for approximately 1 hour until a skewer inserted into the middle comes out clean.

Once baked, remove the cake from the oven and poke it all over with a skewer (but do not poke it all the way through). Put the remaining fruit in a bowl with the granulated sugar and 1 tablespoon of citrus juice. Mix the fruit, sugar and juice together, mashing some of the fruit gently as you go whilst leaving some pieces whole. Add a little more juice, if required, then spoon the mixture over the cake, allowing the juices to run into the cake and the fruit to pile on top.

MUM'S RASPBERRY JAM

During the summer months, Mum is always making jam with raspberries from the garden. It's sweet, a little sharp, and absolutely delicious on Mum's Scones (see page 30) or in our Viennese Whirls (see page 100). If you're using raspberries from the garden, make sure to get rid of any leaves and bugs! You can also strain the jam through a sieve or fine muslin before putting it into jars if you prefer your jam without seeds.

Makes: 700g (approx.)
Prep time: 5 minutes
Cooking time: 20 minutes

500g ripe raspberries, washed (you can also use blackberries or blueberries for this recipe)
1 unwaxed lemon
500g jam sugar with added pectin

Put two or three heatproof plates in the freezer – these will be used later to test the jam's setting point.

Sterilise your jars by washing them in hot, soapy water and drying them out in a low oven.

Add the raspberries to a heavy-bottomed pan and mash gently with a wooden spoon.

Cut the lemon in half, squeeze the juice into the pan, and add the skin of the lemon.

Add the sugar and heat to a rolling boil, stirring occasionally to distribute the sugar. Boil for about 10 minutes.

Turn down the heat and scoop a teaspoon of jam onto one of the chilled plates before putting it in the fridge for 1 to 2 minutes. Push your finger or the end of a spoon though the jam, and if the jam wrinkles, it has reached its setting point. If it is not yet ready, boil for a few more minutes before testing again on another chilled plate.

Once the jam has reached its setting point, remove the lemon and use a spoon to carefully remove any scum from the top of the jam. This can be added to your compost.

All to cool for 5 minutes before pouring carefully into the sterilised jars – this will ensure the raspberry seeds are evenly distributed, but the jam will still be hot enough to be sterile. Take care to wipe any jam from the rim as it will prevent the jars sealing and reduce the shelf life.

Put the lids on while the jam's still hot and allow to cool fully before storing in a cool dark place. The jam will keep unopened for up to a year. Once opened, keep it in the fridge.

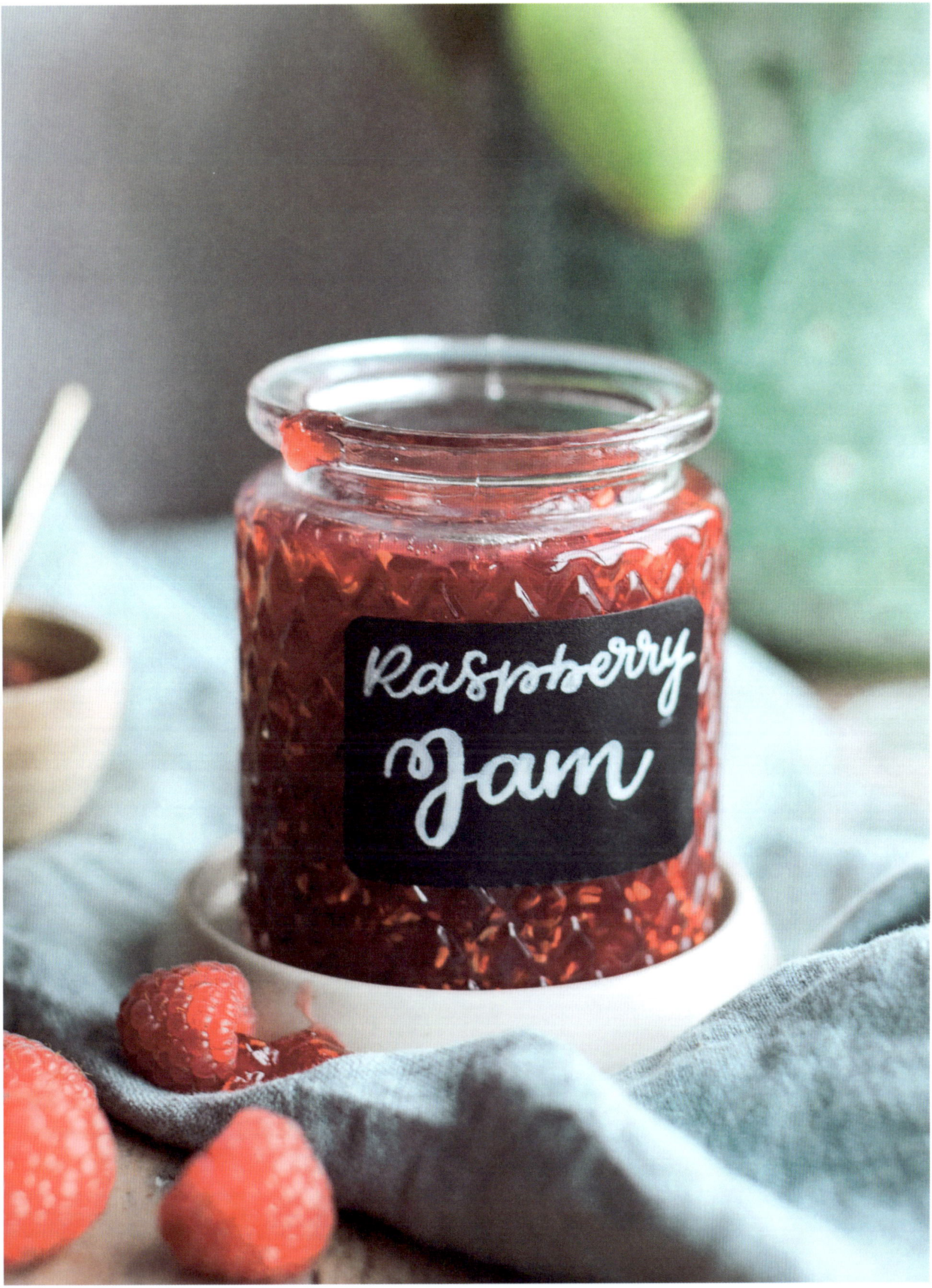
Raspberry
Jam

FOOD WASTE

"WE DON'T NEED A HANDFUL OF PEOPLE
DOING ZERO WASTE PERFECTLY. WE NEED
MILLIONS OF PEOPLE DOING IT IMPERFECTLY."

– ANNE MARIE BONNEAU

WHY DOES FOOD WASTE MATTER?

Over 10 million tonnes of food are wasted in the UK each year, the cost of which is both financially and environmentally huge. 70% of this could have been eaten, which equates to 15 billion meals, and this wasted food equates to 8-10% of man-made greenhouse gas emissions. To put this into context, aviation only contributes 2.5%. By weight, 60% of this food waste comes from households (source: WRAP, The Waste and Resources Action Programme).

PLASTIC WASTE

Microplastics have been found everywhere, from the bottom of the ocean to our brains, and a plastic 'island' three times the size of France is floating in the North Pacific. Somehow, humans need to reduce the amount of plastic produced and used in everyday life. The best thing to do with plastic that is already in circulation is to reuse it, and recycle it when it's at the end of its life. Recycling is resource intensive, and a lot that goes into recycling schemes ends up in landfill or is incinerated, so it should be considered a last resort and not a solution. When baking, we can aim to buy food that has less plastic packaging, perhaps grow our own, use refill shops, buy from markets and farm shops, and, if none of the above are possible, try buying the items with the least amount of plastic packaging.

BUY WHAT YOU NEED

By only buying what we need and preserving, storing, and using all of it, we can make a real change. Be sure to use what you already have. Plenty of the recipes in this book can be adapted; for example, if a bake calls for raspberries, you could try blackberries or strawberries instead. If you still have excess, offer it to family, friends or others – we love the app Olio for sharing spare food with neighbours.

STORE FOOD CORRECTLY

Ensure that you store food according to the proper instructions – this will prolong its shelf life and help prevent waste.

COMMONLY WASTED FOOD
AND HOW TO AVOID IT

MILK AND BREAD

Milk and bread are two of the most wasted products in the UK, but it doesn't need to be that way! Milk can be frozen (don't freeze in glass), and trust us when we say sour milk makes the most delicious fluffy scones (page 30), pancakes (page 26), and waffles. It can also be used in place of buttermilk or sour cream in baking and cooking.

Our Chocolate Stale Bread Cake (page 78) and Breadcrumb Plum Cake (page 74) turn 'waste' into something delicious. Breadcrumbs can also be used to replace flour in denser bakes such as carrot and fruit cakes. Brioche and white bread is ideal for Edward's Chocolate French Toast (see page 90) and bread pudding. Stale bread can also be crumbed and frozen ready for baking or creating crispy toppings on sweet and savoury dishes. Experiment and see what works for you!

EGGS

Eggs last well beyond their best before date. If you are not sure how fresh they are, try the float test. If an egg floats in a glass of water, then it's gone off. If it sinks, it's fresh. Eggs that stand up in water are fine to use in baking but are less fresh, so use these up first.

FRUIT

Fruit can be frozen, dried, or preserved by making jam, curd, or being bottled. Lightly stewed fruit freezes well, and soft fruits such as blackberries and currants can be frozen fresh to be cooked later. We love River Cottage's fruit preserving recipes.

CAKES AND BISCUITS

Many cakes can be frozen and defrosted as required. Usually, it's better to freeze them without icing if possible, although this is only because they look better freshly iced. Any scrappy bits of stale cake or biscuits can be frozen until you have enough to make something, such as Tiffin (page 40) or Refrigerator Cake (page 150). Soft biscuits will also re-crisp in a very low oven.

PEELINGS

Apple skins brushed with butter, sprinkled with cinnamon sugar, and baked make delicious crisps. The same can be done with vegetable peel and a little salt. See our Apple Scrap Jelly recipe (page 158) for using up apple cores and peel.

BEST BEFORE DATES

These are simply a guide; use your eyes, nose, taste, and common sense to decide if something is still edible or not. Very often, it will be!

COMPOSTING

There will, of course, always be some food waste, and when all that possibly can be eaten has been, you'll need to do something with the rest. If composting is an option, either at home or through your council, it's a great planet friendly option. Under current legislation, all councils in England will have to collect food waste by 31st March 2026, and Wales and Scotland already offer this service. They will provide a bin if you do not have one. At home, compost is incredibly useful if you have a garden or potted plants. There's no need to worry about it being smelly or gross! There's a lot of information online and in books about how to compost, and it really isn't too complicated as long as you add a mixture of elements, such as cardboard, alongside garden clippings and food waste.

PACKAGING

Much of what we buy is pre-packaged in single-use packaging. Some of this cannot be avoided, but taking steps to reduce this has a hugely positive environmental impact when you consider that 70,000 tonnes of hard-to-recycle plastics are used just to package uncut fruit and veg each year.

REDUCE

Greengrocers and farm shops generally have far less plastic and other packaging on their products. Refill shops are becoming more and more readily available, so do use them where you can. Every purchase will help support these fantastic initiatives, put money into your local economy, and be better for the planet.

REUSE

From bread bags to takeaway tubs, much of the packaging we have in our homes can be reused for leftovers, sandwiches, or freezing fruit. You can use tin foil many times as a wrap and even use a clean shower cap as a bowl cover when proving dough. Cling film can easily be washed and reused – when it's wet, it doesn't stick to itself!

Think carefully and creatively before throwing anything out; you might be surprised with the uses you can come up with. We used to use baking parchment for every bake until we realised that greasing and dusting the tin with flour or cocoa powder normally works just as well.

We have invested in reusable silicone sheets and we've cut these to size for our favourite baking trays and tins, which removes the need for any baking parchment. When we recommend silicone sheets or baking parchment in this book, it is needed for the bake to work properly, but do reuse wherever you can!

AS A LAST RESORT, RECYCLE

In the UK, 90 billion plastic items are disposed of each year. Only 17% of this is recycled, with the remainder ending up in landfill. Much of what we add to our recycling bin is not actually recycled at all. This is due to our systems simply not being able to cope with the huge amount of plastic that is generated. For this reason, plastic should only be used as a last resort, hence the motto: reduce, reuse, recycle.

AUTUMN

As summer fades, autumn rolls in and brings with it a wonderful light and a cosy feel. We wake up to misty mornings, carpets of colourful leaves, and hedgerows full of berries, all bathed in golden light.

Some British fruit is only now fully ripening; apples and pears come into their own, figs sweeten, and blackberries still adorn the hedgerows. If you enjoy foraging, elderberries are now ready to pick. To make an immune-boosting syrup, pick plump elderberries, separate them from their stalks, and simmer in 1cm of water for about 20 minutes, then strain and measure the liquid. Add an equal amount of sugar to the liquid, return to the pan, and bubble again until the sugar has dissolved. Once cool, keep in the fridge for up to three months; drink a little whenever you feel a cold coming on.

It's the time of year when we think of making sweet tarts and pies and eating fruit crumble with hot custard. There's still some warmth outside, and we might yet be able to sit, with a coffee and a slice of something sweet, in a spot warmed by the autumn sun. Vegetables such as pumpkins and beetroot are in abundance and are wonderful in cakes, adding a depth of flavour and maybe a bit more nutrition! If you carve a pumpkin at Halloween, save the flesh for a Pumpkin Spice Cake (page 148). The seeds can be washed and roasted with sea salt and they are wonderful on top of a thick vegetable soup. This month also calls for chocolate; when picking out bars at the shop, aim for fairtrade with a high cocoa content.

FRENCH APPLE TART

I'm always happy when apple season arrives and it's time to bake with all the varieties you can find in people's gardens. There always seems to be some going spare. An apple tart is simple and delicious, and this one is layered with frangipane and topped with caramelised apples. I think it's best warm, but others love a slice once cooled.

Makes: 1 large 9-inch tart
Prep time: 45 minutes, plus 1 hour chilling
Cooking time: 1 hour
Oven temp: 180°C fan

FOR THE PASTRY

130g cold, salted butter

200g plain flour

1 tbsp caster sugar

1 egg, beaten (or 40-50ml of water)

FOR THE FILLING

10 eating apples (approx.)

60g golden caster sugar

½ tsp ground cinnamon

½ tsp mixed spice

30g butter, melted

3 tbsp seedless jam (such as apricot)

To make the pastry, rub the butter into the flour and sugar until it resembles breadcrumbs. Try to use your fingertips so the butter doesn't get too warm. Mix in the egg or water and gently knead until it forms a dough. When it comes together, form it into a small, thick disc, cover with airtight reusable food wrap, and chill in the fridge for at least an hour.

Roll the pastry out into a circle until it is the thickness of a £1 coin then line a 9-inch tart case, making sure to push the pastry into the grooves. Prick the bottom several times with a fork before lining with baking parchment and filling with baking beans, or uncooked rice or lentils.

Bake for 15 minutes, then remove the paper and beans, rice, or lentils and bake for another 10 minutes until the pastry looks biscuity. It needs to be cooked but not too dark as it will be cooked again with the filling.

Whilst the pastry is cooking, peel, core and chop all but four of the apples (these will be used for the top). Put the chopped apples in a saucepan with 1 tablespoon of water and 45g of the sugar. Cook on a low heat, stirring every few minutes, until they form a soft purée. If it seems dry and is catching on the pan, add another tablespoon of water. Stir in the cinnamon and mixed spice.

Peel, quarter, core and thinly slice the remaining apples. Spread the apple purée over the pastry base, then arrange the apple slices on top. Start on the outside and overlap each slice slightly as they will shrink as they cook. Brush the apples with melted butter and sprinkle over the remaining sugar.

Bake for 25 to 30 minutes until golden. Do check on the tart, and if it looks like some apples or the edges of the pastry are browning too quickly, put a heavy baking tray on the shelf just above. This helps disperse the heat so it can cook evenly without browning.

When the tart is baked, remove it from the oven. Whilst still hot, mix the jam with a little freshly boiled water until it is just runny enough to brush over the apples. Glaze the tart with the jam and allow to cool a little before removing from the tin.

Serve warm or cold, and on its own or with a scoop of vanilla ice cream.

ISABELLA'S CHOCOLATE MUG CAKE

My daughter, Isabella, says: "A teenager's best friend, this mug cake is easy, quick, and delicious. It's perfect for those times when nothing but chocolate will do! I make one of these at least once a week, but the most annoying thing about it is when I make one, everyone else wants one, too!"

Makes: 1
Prep time: 10 minutes
Cooking time: 2 minutes

4 tbsp self-raising flour
4 tbsp caster sugar
2 tbsp cocoa powder
3 tbsp milk
3 tbsp sunflower oil
1 egg
A small handful of white chocolate chips
A small handful of dark chocolate chips

Add all the ingredients to a large mug and mix well with a fork until combined.

Microwave for 2 to 2 and a half minutes, depending on the microwave's wattage. Check after 2 minutes before any extra cooking time. When ready, the cake will look soft but not runny – be sure to take it out when it still looks undercooked.

Let it stand for 1 minute to finish cooking in the mug's residual heat.

Sprinkle with more chocolate chips, then enjoy warm straight from the mug.

ISABELLA'S TIP
Try adding a scoop of ice cream on top for an extra yummy treat!

BERRY AND ALMOND CAKE

A quick, delicious, and adaptable recipe, this cake lends itself to any berries you have to hand. We use raspberries, but blackberries, blueberries, strawberries, or other soft fruit also work perfectly well. You can also make it in muffin cases instead of one large cake.

Serves: 12
Prep time: 10 minutes
Cooking time: 45-50 minutes
Oven temp: 160°C fan

140g ground almonds
140g salted butter, softened
140g caster sugar
140g self-raising flour
2 eggs
1 tsp vanilla or almond extract (optional)
250g berries
2 tbsp flaked almonds
1 tbsp demerara sugar
Icing sugar, for dusting

Grease and flour an 8-inch springform cake tin.

Using an electric whisk, or a wooden spoon and some elbow grease, mix together the ground almonds, butter, caster sugar, flour, eggs, and vanilla or almond extract (if using) until well combined. You can also use a food processor if you wish.

Spread half the cake batter into the tin, then dot the berries over the top. Distribute the rest of the batter over the berries – you may need to blob it on and spread it with a spoon or your fingers. Do your best, but don't worry too much about it being perfectly even as it will spread in the oven.

Sprinkle the flaked almonds and demerara sugar over the top and bake for 45 to 50 minutes until golden.

Leave to cool in the tin before removing and dusting with icing sugar to serve.

ANDREW'S HAZELNUT AND FIG CAKE

Andrew, my brother-in-law, says: "During lockdown, our children decided they would like to give their mum, Laura, a special day in the garden. This called for a delicious cake made with jammy figs, fresh from the garden. The figs work wonderfully with the hazelnut in the sponge, making this cake a firm family favourite."

Serves: 8
Prep time: 45 minutes
Cooking time: 30 minutes
Oven temp: 160°C fan

200g hazelnuts
150g caster sugar
150g salted butter
3 eggs
100ml whole milk
200g self-raising flour
1 tsp baking powder
1 tsp vanilla extract

FOR THE FILLING
200g double cream
1 tsp vanilla extract
4 ripe figs
1 tbsp icing sugar, plus a little extra for dusting

Grease and thoroughly dust two 8-inch round cake tins with flour.

Spread the hazelnuts out evenly on a baking tray and bake for approximately 15 minutes until they start to turn brown. Keep an eye on them: you want them lightly roasted not burnt, otherwise they'll become bitter! Remove them from the oven and let them cool for a few minutes.

Using a food processor or blender, blitz the nuts with approximately one third of the caster sugar until the nuts are finely ground and well combined with the sugar. Transfer to a bowl and set aside.

Add the remaining sugar and the butter to the processor and mix until combined. You can also do this with a handheld whisk.

Add the eggs one at a time until everything is well combined, then add the milk, flour, baking powder and vanilla. Continue mixing until you have a smooth batter.

Add the ground sugar and nuts to the batter and mix until just combined. Divide the cake batter evenly between the prepared tins and bake for 25 to 30 minutes until risen and a light golden colour. Check they are fully baked by inserting a thin metal skewer into the cake - if it comes out clean the cakes are baked. Transfer the tins to a wire rack to cool.

Meanwhile, to make the filling, whisk the cream with the icing sugar and vanilla extract until fully whipped and thickened. Slice each fig into six or eight slices.

Once completely cooled, remove the cakes from the tins. Sandwich the cakes with the cream and the figs, placing the fig slices between two layers of cream to stop the figs making the cake soggy (if you're going to keep it for a day or two). Dust the top of the cake with a little icing sugar to serve.

ANDREW'S TIP
Figs are at their best at the very end of summer, but you could use other fruit instead. A rhubarb jam or blackberries plucked from the hedgerows also work wonderfully.

APPLE BUNDT CAKE
WITH BROWN BUTTER ICING

A bundt cake always makes for a stunning centrepiece. The trick is to ensure every nook and cranny is greased and dusted to prevent sticking. Don't panic if it does stick, as any mishaps in this delicious autumnal version can be covered with the decadent icing.

Serves: 12
Prep time: 40 minutes, plus 1 hour cooling
Cooking time: 1 hour
Oven temp: 160°C fan

FOR THE CAKE
285g vegetable oil
400g caster sugar
1 tsp vanilla extract
3 eggs
360g plain flour
1 tsp bicarbonate of soda
1 tsp salt
1 tsp ground cinnamon
½ tsp ground ginger
350g eating apples, peeled, cored and chopped

FOR THE ICING
200g salted butter, cubed
300g icing sugar
½ tsp ground cinnamon

YOU WILL NEED
Piping bag with a 1cm tip

FOR THE CAKE

Thoroughly grease a bundt tin, being careful to cover the entire surface so the cake does not stick and lose the pattern or shape when it is released. Dust with 2 tablespoons of flour, tipping the tin on its side and gently tapping it whilst turning until it is covered in a thin layer of flour. To remove the excess, turn the tin upside down and tap gently.

In the bowl of a stand mixer, add the oil, sugar and vanilla extract. Beat on a medium speed for 3 to 4 minutes until the mixture is light and fluffy. Add the eggs and mix until well combined and smooth.

Sift in the dry ingredients and mix briefly before adding the chopped apples. Mix on a low speed for 2 minutes until well combined.

Pour the batter evenly into the bundt tin, rotating the tin slowly as you pour to distribute it evenly. Use a spoon to smooth the top, then bake the cake for 50 minutes to an hour until golden brown and a skewer inserted into the centre comes out clean. Take care to check that any residue on the skewer is batter not apple – if it is only apple, the cake will be cooked.

Allow the cake to cool in the tin for 5 minutes, then turn it out onto a wire rack. Wait until the cake is cooled to room temperature before making the icing.

FOR THE ICING

To make the icing, heat the butter over a medium heat until browned and foaming. Keep an eye on it as you want it golden brown, not burnt. When the butter has melted, take it off the heat and leave to cool for a few minutes. Add the icing sugar and cinnamon and mix well.

Transfer the icing to a piping bag with a 1cm opening or tip and pipe over the cake in a back and forth motion from the centre to the outside, going all around the cake. The icing will harden as it cools, so work fairly quickly to ensure the icing falls evenly and sets as it drips over the side of the cake.

BAKER'S TIP

If you'd like to make a plant-based browned butter, use 200g of a plant-based butter block and add 2 teaspoons of smooth nut butter. Melt over a low heat, whisking constantly, until it foams and browns, but do keep a close eye on it so it doesn't burn!

CARROT CAKE COOKIES

A slightly different take on a carrot cake, these cookies are warming, wholesome and delicious. They were one of our subscription bakes, and they were very popular!

Makes: 8
Prep time: 30 minutes
Cooking time: 12-15 minutes
Oven temp: 180°C fan

FOR THE COOKIES

70g salted butter, softened

100g light soft brown sugar

65g carrot, grated

1 egg

125 self-raising flour

20g oats

½ tsp ground cinnamon

½ tsp mixed spice

30g raisins

25g walnuts, chopped (1 tbsp set aside, to decorate)

FOR THE ICING

60g icing sugar

2 tbsp milk

¼ tsp vanilla extract

20g full-fat cream cheese

FOR THE TOPPING

½ orange, zested

1 tbsp reserved chopped walnuts

Line two baking trays with reusable silicone sheets or baking parchment.

In a large mixing bowl, use an electric mixer to beat the butter and sugar together until light and fluffy.

Add the grated carrot, egg, flour, oats, cinnamon, mixed spice and raisins. Add the chopped walnuts, making sure 1 tablespoon is set aside for the topping. Stir together until well combined.

Use your hands to roll the mixture into eight equal balls and place four on each prepared tray. The mixture will be sticky, so oil the back of a dessert spoon to flatten each ball slightly (they will flatten further as they bake).

Bake for 12 to 15 minutes, rotating the trays halfway through, until the cookies are golden brown around the edges. Remove from the oven and transfer to a wire rack to cool completely.

Once cooled, prepare the icing. Sift the icing sugar into a bowl and add the milk and vanilla extract. Mix until smooth, then stir in the cream cheese until just combined (be careful not to overmix as it may split).

Using a spoon, drizzle the icing over the cookies, then sprinkle over the orange zest and reserved walnuts. Leave the icing to harden before serving.

APPLE AND DATE HAND PIES

A really fun way to make pies without needing a pie tin. The decoration is optional but makes for a really unusual dessert.

Makes: 8
Prep time: 1 hour, plus 1 hour 15 minutes chilling
Cooking time: 20 minutes
Oven temp: 180°C fan

FOR THE PASTRY

360g plain flour

50g caster sugar

230g cold, salted butter, cubed

4 tbsp cold water

FOR THE FILLING

4 Granny Smith apples, peeled, cored, and chopped into 1 cm chunks

1 orange, zested and juiced

½ tsp ground cinnamon

4 tbsp light soft brown sugar

12 dates, pitted and chopped

1 tbsp cornflour

2-4 tbsp water

FOR THE DECORATION

Beaten egg, or milk, to seal and glaze

1 tbsp water

½ tsp red food colouring powder or paste

½ tsp yellow food colouring powder or paste

YOU WILL NEED

Cookie cutters or a paper template

Line two baking trays with reusable silicone sheets or baking parchment.

To make the pastry, combine the flour and sugar in a mixing bowl. Add the cubed butter and use the tips of your fingers to rub the ingredients together until the mixture resembles coarse breadcrumbs.

Add the water and knead until the mixture comes together to form a ball of dough. Divide the dough into two portions, flatten each into a thick disc, then wrap them individually in reusable food wrap or a bag (an old bread bag is ideal!). Chill in the fridge for 1 hour.

To prepare the filling, place the chopped apple into a small saucepan with the orange zest and juice, cinnamon, and brown sugar. Gently simmer over a medium heat for 6 to 8 minutes until the apples are almost tender, adding a little water if needed. Add the chopped dates and stir.

Mix the cornflour and 2 tablespoons of cold water in a cup then add it to the apples and stir to combine. Cook for 1 more minute before removing from the heat and leaving to cool.

Line two baking trays with baking parchment. Place one of the pastry discs on a floured surface and roll it into a rectangle about 2-3mm thick. If you wish, use scissors to cut a leaf template approx. 12 x 15cm; alternatively, you can use a cookie cutter of a design of your liking or use your hands to shape the pastry. Using a sharp knife, cut eight shapes of a similar size (or they will not bake evenly), rerolling if needed. Transfer each shape to the baking trays, four on each, and chill them in the fridge. Roll the second piece of dough and cut the shapes out again so you have eight identical pairs.

Mix the beaten egg with 1 tablespoon of cold water in a cup and set aside. Remove the baking trays from the fridge and spoon the pie filling into the centres of the shapes, distributing it evenly. Brush the egg wash or milk around the rim of the pastry before topping with another matching shape and gently pushing down to make sure it adheres. Use a fork to gently crimp the edges together. Repeat with the remaining pies and return to the fridge for 15 minutes. Keep the remaining egg wash to glaze later.

If using, put a little food colouring powder or paste on opposite sides of a plate and fill a glass with water. Once the pies have chilled, paint the surfaces using a clean paintbrush (you can dip the brush in water and mix with the food colouring powders or paste to make edible paint). Leave to dry for a few minutes then glaze the pies with the remaining egg wash.

Finally, poke a fork into the surface of each pie to allow steam to escape and bake for 20 minutes until the pies are golden. Leave to cool before serving.

BAKER'S TIP

Use the peelings and cores from the apple to make crisps or Apple Scrap Jelly (see page 158).

Scan for template

PECAN PIE CRUFFINS

Cruffins are simply croissants made in a muffin tin, and they usually have a delicious filling. These pecan pie-inspired cruffins make for a very indulgent bake, and they're perfect with a cup of coffee. This recipe will double easily, if desired.

Makes: 6
Prep time: 1 hour 45 minutes, plus 18 hours proving/chilling
Cooking time: 20 minutes
Oven temp: 180°C fan

FOR THE DOUGH

200g strong white bread flour
¼ tsp salt
20g caster sugar
1 tsp instant yeast
140ml warm water
120g salted butter, softened

FOR THE PECAN PRALINE

50g caster sugar
1 tbsp water
50 pecans, chopped

FOR THE ICING

50g salted butter, softened
100g icing sugar
1 tbsp milk

YOU WILL NEED

Piping bag with a 1cm tip

FOR THE DOUGH

In a large mixing bowl, or in a stand mixer with a dough hook attached, combine the flour, salt, caster sugar, yeast and water. Knead for 10 minutes, or until the dough is smooth and elastic. Transfer the dough to a lightly oiled bowl, cover with a clean, damp tea towel or shower cap and leave to rise in a warm place for 1 hour or until doubled in size.

Meanwhile, place the butter between two sheets of baking parchment and use a rolling pin to bash and roll it – take your time with this step as it's important to break down the butter. Shape the butter into a rectangle, about 20x15cm. Leave it wrapped in the paper and put it in the fridge to chill.

Put the ball of dough on a floured work surface and roll it out into a rectangle approximately 30x20cm. Shape the corners by pulling the dough out with your hands. If the dough shrinks back to an oval, put it in the fridge for 10 minutes before trying again. Unwrap the slab of butter and place it in the middle of the dough, leaving equal amounts of dough on either side.

Fold one side of the dough halfway over the butter, then take the other side of the dough and fold it over the butter in the same way so the edges of the dough meet in the middle. Fold in half along the line where the dough meets, then wrap in reusable food wrap and place in the fridge for 30 minutes.

Repeat the rolling, folding and chilling process twice more, re-rolling the dough whilst still folded without adding more butter. If the butter breaks through the surface of the dough at any point, don't worry, just dust it with a little flour and continue. In between chilling steps, prepare the praline.

FOR THE PECAN PRALINE

Line a baking tray with baking parchment and set aside. In a small pan, combine the sugar and water and warm over a low heat, swirling the pan until the sugar has dissolved. Increase the heat to high and boil until the mixture turns amber. Remove from the heat and add the chopped pecans, stirring quickly to coat the nuts, then tip out onto the prepared tray. Leave to cool and harden until later.

FOR THE BAKE

Carefully roll the dough out into a rectangle, neatly trim the edges, then cut the dough into three equal rectangles. Starting at a longer edge, tightly roll each rectangle into a cylinder, like a Swiss roll. Cut each roll lengthwise along the seam with a sharp knife so you have six lengths of layered dough in total. Roll each length into a spiral, cut side up, and place into a muffin tin. Cover the tin loosely with a damp tea towel and leave to rise for 1 hour at room temperature (18-24°C). Once risen, bake in the centre of the oven for 20 minutes until risen and golden brown. Remove from the oven and place on a wire rack to cool.

FOR THE ICING

Break the praline into pieces with a rolling pin and reserve 1 tablespoon for later. Transfer the remaining praline to a blender and blitz until fine. In a mixing bowl, beat the butter until creamy, add the icing sugar and continue to beat until light and fluffy. Add the ground praline and milk then mix to combine. Spoon the mixture into a piping bag and tie a knot in the opening. Snip 1cm from the tip of the piping bag or use a piping tip with a 1cm hole, and top each cruffin with icing. Finish with a sprinkling of the reserved praline. Enjoy!

BEETROOT BROWNIES

This is one of the only ways I can get my kids to eat beetroot, and they've still not guessed the secret ingredient!

Makes: 12
Prep time: 30 minutes
Cooking time: 45 minutes
Oven temp: 160°C fan

500g whole raw beetroots
100g salted butter, cubed
200g dark chocolate, chopped
2 tsp vanilla extract
250g golden caster sugar
3 eggs
75g plain flour
50g cocoa powder

Grease an 30x20cm baking tin and dust with cocoa powder. Weight out any excess cocoa to use in the brownie.

Cut the tops and tails off the beetroot (you can eat the beetroot greens – they are similar to spinach). Chop the beetroot into chunks and place in a microwavable bowl – you may want to wear gloves to prevent staining your hands! Add a little water and microwave on high for 10 to 12 minutes until tender.

When cooked, drain the excess water before transferring the beetroot to a bowl with the butter, dark chocolate and vanilla. Blend with a stick blender (or in a food processor); the chocolate and butter will melt with the heat of the blender and beetroot and the ingredients will gradually combine.

In a separate bowl, whisk the sugar and eggs with an electric hand whisk for a few minutes until pale and foamy. Add the beetroot mix to the eggs and fold through with a spoon, taking care not to lose too much air.

Sift in the flour and cocoa powder (sifting incorporates more air and stops the brownie being too heavy) then fold into the batter until well combined.

Pour the brownie batter into the tin and bake for 25 to 30 minutes until it has risen all over. When cooked, the brownie will have a crust and a very slight ripple in the centre when the tin is lightly shaken.

Cool completely in the tin before removing and cutting into squares.

BANANA CHOCOLATE LOAF

This classic banana cake is elevated by the addition of chocolate. We challenge you to make this and not devour it as soon as it is cool enough to eat! Bananas get sweeter as they ripen, so the softer they are, the better. If you have bananas that are going over but do not have time to bake, peel them and pop them in the freezer in a tub or bag until you are ready (an old bread bag is perfect!). The bananas will be even softer when they defrost but they are perfectly fine to use.

Makes: 1 loaf
Prep time: 10 minutes
Cooking time: 1 hour
Oven temp: 170°C fan

4 tbsp cocoa powder
4 ripe bananas, peeled
250g golden caster sugar
2 eggs
140g butter, softened
250g plain flour
2 tsp baking powder
100g milk chocolate chips
100g white chocolate chips
250g chocolate spread

Grease a 3lb loaf tin and dust the base and sides well with cocoa powder.

In a large bowl, mash together the bananas and sugar. Add the eggs and mix well before adding the butter for a final mix.

Sift in the flour and baking powder and fold it through until combined. Stir in the chocolate chips until evenly distributed.

Pour the batter into the loaf tin and bake in the oven for 1 hour. The loaf will be baked when a clean knife or skewer inserted into the middle comes out clean. Leave to cool on a wire rack before removing from the tin.

Once cool, pop onto a serving tray and slather on a generous amount of chocolate spread, sweeping your knife from left to right to create a gorgeous icing. Sprinkle the top with a few extra chocolate chips for a little extra jazz!

CHOCOLATE AND HAZELNUT BABKA KNOTS

I really enjoy making these, especially the plaiting and shaping! Usually, I start making these in the afternoon and prove them overnight so we can have them fresh for breakfast. If you're feeling creative, try swapping the filling for other flavours, such as apple and cinnamon.

Makes: 9
Prep time: 2 hours, plus 4-5 hours proving
Cooking time: 25-30 minutes
Oven temp: 160°C fan

FOR THE CHOCOLATE AND HAZELNUT FILLING

70g roasted hazelnuts, finely chopped, plus extra to garnish

100g dark chocolate

1 tbsp icing sugar

1 tbsp whole milk powder

150ml single cream

FOR THE DOUGH

450g strong white bread flour

7g instant yeast

70g caster sugar

½ tsp salt

280ml warm milk

30g butter, melted

1 egg yolk

FOR THE GLAZE

20g caster sugar

20ml water

½ tsp vanilla extract

½ tbsp hazelnuts, chopped

FOR THE CHOCOLATE AND HAZELNUT FILLING

Grind the hazelnuts down to a smooth paste in a food processor. Depending on your machine, this will take about 10 minutes, and you'll need to keep scraping down the sides. Be careful the motor doesn't overheat.

Meanwhile, melt the chocolate in a heatproof bowl set over, but not touching, a pan of simmering water. Add the icing sugar, milk powder, and cream and heat to a simmer.

Remove from the heat and stir in the hazelnut paste. Allow to cool, then place in the fridge until ready to fill the babka.

FOR THE DOUGH

Combine the flour, yeast, caster sugar and salt in a large mixing bowl. Make a well in the centre of the dry ingredients and add the warm milk, melted butter, and egg yolk. Mix everything together to form a dough.

Turn the dough out onto a floured surface and knead for 10 minutes or until the dough is smooth and elastic. You can also do this with a stand mixer with a dough hook attachment.

Place the ball of dough in a lightly oiled bowl and cover with a damp towel or clean shower cap. Leave to prove in a warm place for 1 hour or until doubled in size.

Once risen, turn the dough out onto a floured surface and roll out into a large rectangle. Spread the chocolate filling over two thirds of the dough (fig. 1). Next, fold the uncovered third of dough towards the middle, then the other end of the dough on top of that, like you are folding a letter (fig. 2). Using a pizza cutter or sharp knife, straighten the ends of the rectangle (fig. 3).

Cut the dough widthways into nine strips, approximately 4cm wide, and gently flatten the strips of dough with your hand. Make two cuts down the length of each strip, leaving them attached at one end, each strip of dough should have three strands (fig. 4).

Plait each strip (fig. 5), then roll them up to create a knot (fig. 6). Transfer the buns to a lightly greased 12-hole muffin tin, cover with a damp tea towel, and leave to rise for 1 hour or in the fridge overnight. If proving in the fridge, remove the buns from the fridge for 30 to 45 mins before you bake them.

Bake the buns for 15 to 20 minutes until a deep golden-brown. Remove from the oven and allow to cool for 10 minutes.

FOR THE GLAZE

In a small pan, combine the caster sugar and water. Bring to a simmer and cook for 2 to 3 minutes. Remove from the heat and add the vanilla extract. Brush the syrup over the warm buns and finish with a sprinkling of chopped hazelnuts.

BAKER'S TIP

A pre-made chocolate spread works well for the filling if you are short of time. If you complete the second prove in the fridge overnight, you can then bake these in the morning for an indulgent breakfast.

fig. 1

fig. 2

fig. 3

fig. 4

fig. 5

fig. 6

CHOCOLATE CHIP COOKIES

Easy to bake and incredibly moreish, these cookies are a staple in any Honeywell household! They are the perfect combination of a crispy edges and soft centre and are so delicious when still warm. This recipe uses a whole tin of condensed milk, which does make a lot of cookies – if there are too many, roll them into balls, slightly flatten the tops, then freeze them in a tub or bag. They can be baked straight from frozen – just pop them on a baking tray and bake as usual, adding approximately 5 minutes to the cooking time.

Makes: 50
Prep time: 10 minutes
Cooking time: 15-20 minutes
Oven temp: 160°C fan

450g butter, softened
450g caster sugar
1 x 397g tin of condensed milk
700g self-raising flour
350g chocolate chunks or chips of your choice

In a large bowl, use a wooden spoon to cream the butter and sugar together.

Add the condensed milk and mix well before adding the flour. Mix to a soft dough, using your hands to bring the ingredients together. Fold in the chocolate until evenly distributed.

To make the cookies, roll the dough into 50 even balls, then flatten them slightly and place on a lined baking tray. Leave 5-6cm around each one to allow for spreading.

Bake for 15 to 20 minutes, making sure to check their colour after 10 minutes. They will be baked when the cookies are slightly golden and still soft (remember they will harden as they cool).

CHOCOLATE AND PEAR HAZELNUT TARTS

Chocolate and pears marry perfectly in this autumnal bake, and the addition of chocolate pastry makes it extra tasty. This recipe uses two eggs: beat them together, set aside 35g for the dough, then use the remaining for the filling.

Makes: 1 large or 6 small tarts
Prep time: 50 minutes, plus 30 minutes chilling
Cooking time: 1 hour
Oven temp: Pastry case: 180°C fan;
Filling: 160°C fan

FOR THE PASTRY

150g plain flour

1 tbsp cocoa powder

40g caster sugar

75g cold butter, cubed

35g beaten egg

FOR THE FILLING

100g roasted hazelnuts

75g butter, softened

75g caster sugar

50g beaten egg

1 tbsp plain flour

1 tbsp cocoa powder

FOR THE TOPPING

3 pears

1 tbsp light soft brown sugar

1 tbsp icing sugar, for dusting

FOR THE PASTRY

Combine the flour, cocoa powder and sugar in a mixing bowl. Add the cubed butter and use the tips of your fingers to rub the ingredients together until the mixture resembles breadcrumbs.

Add the beaten egg and knead until it comes together to form a ball of dough. Wrap in baking parchment or transfer to a bag and chill for 30 minutes.

Grease six individual tart tins or one 8-inch tart tin with butter and dust with a little flour.

On a floured surface, roll the chilled pastry dough into a circle approximately 3-4mm thick. If using small tins, cut the pasty into circles slightly larger than the tins to create some overhang and allow for shrinkage. Re-roll the pastry as necessary. Press the pastry into the tin/s, carefully pushing it into the edges.

Prick the base of the pastry with a fork a few times and bake for 15 minutes at 180°C fan.

FOR THE FILLING

Blitz the hazelnuts in a food processor until smooth and creamy, like peanut butter. This can take some time, so be patient! Whisk together the butter, sugar and egg until light and smooth, then add the hazelnut paste, flour and cocoa powder. Stir until combined, then set aside.

FOR THE TOPPING AND BAKE

Peel the pears, slice in half lengthwise, and remove the cores. Place cut side down on a chopping board and cut slits into pears about 2mm apart, being careful not to go all the way through so they are still attached along the cut edge.

Spoon the hazelnut filling into the pastry case/s and spread it out evenly, leaving some space at the top to prevent the tarts from overflowing as they bake. Arrange the pears on top and sprinkle with a little brown sugar.

Bake the pies at 160°C fan for 35 to 45 minutes until the pears are golden and the filling is no longer wobbly. Leave to cool before removing from the tin/s. Dust with icing sugar before serving.

GRANDMA HONEY'S 'GRASSMERE GINGERBREAD'

This no-nonsense, sweet, warming bake is a recipe handed down by our wonderful Grandma Honey, my dad's mum. An Irish lady with red curly hair, a booming voice, and a penchant for bright eyeshadow, days with Grandma Honey were always full of fun. This gingerbread is a family favourite, now with the great grandchildren too, and for the adults among us conjures up fond memories of picnics in Grandma Honey's garden under the big beech tree. It is ideal for days out as its dense texture means it holds its shape and doesn't fall apart. The question is always which bit is best: a chewy corner or a softer centre piece?

Makes: 12 squares
Prep time: 20 minutes
Cooking time: 20 minutes
Oven temp: 180°C

170g butter
1 heaped tbsp golden syrup
280g self-raising flour
170g demerara sugar
1 tbsp mixed peel
1 tsp ground ginger

Grease and flour a 20x20cm baking tin – a round tin is perfectly fine to use, you will just need to be creative with your cutting!

Melt the butter and syrup together in a heavy-bottomed saucepan, then stir in the remaining ingredients until well combined.

Press the mixture into the tin, using the back of a spoon to ensure the mixture is evenly distributed.

Bake for 20 minutes until golden.

Once baked, allow to cool for 10 to 15 minutes in the tin before turning it out onto a wire rack or chopping board. Once fully cooled, cut into 12 even squares or slices.

PUMPKIN SPICE CAKE

This cake is soft, warming, and utterly comforting. It is the most perfect autumnal bake, and as an added bonus, it freezes well. You could use other types of squash, but bear in mind the cake will not be as sweet, so you may want to add a little extra sugar. This is best enjoyed with a mug of hot chocolate after a long walk on a chilly autumnal day.

Makes: 24 squares
Prep time: 30 minutes
Cooking time: 35 minutes
Oven temp: 160°C fan

FOR THE CAKE

800g squash or pumpkin

250g plain flour

2 tsp baking powder

1 tsp bicarbonate of soda

1 tsp salt

2 tsp ground cinnamon

½ tsp ground ginger

½ tsp ground nutmeg

1 tsp mixed spice

240ml vegetable oil

4 eggs

200g dark or light soft brown sugar

100g caster sugar

1 tsp vanilla extract

FOR THE ICING

100g butter, softened

350g icing sugar

200g full-fat cream cheese

FOR THE CAKE

Cut the squash in half lengthways and remove the seeds (these can be washed, oiled, salted, and roasted if you wish - they are delicious sprinkled on top of soup!). Place the squash halves cut side up on a plate and microwave for approximately 10 minutes, checking every 2 minutes, until the flesh is soft. Once soft, allow to cool for a few minutes then scrape the flesh into a bowl, weighing out 450g. Do not throw any excess away as it is delicious mashed with carrot or blended into a soup with other roasted veg!

If you do not have a microwave, prepare the squash in the same way then place it on a baking tray and roast at 180°C fan for about 45 minutes.

Grease and flour a brownie tin, 30x20cm – if the pan is bigger or smaller, that's okay, just be aware that a thicker cake will take longer to cook. The pan needs to be around 5cm deep to allow the cake to rise.

Combine the flour, baking powder, bicarbonate of soda, salt and spices in a large bowl. In a separate bowl, whisk the oil, eggs, sugars, squash and vanilla until well combined. Pour the wet ingredients into the dry and whisk or stir until thoroughly mixed. Note: the batter will be thick.

Pour the batter into the prepared tin and bake for 30 to 35 minutes; the cake is done when a metal skewer inserted into the centre comes out clean. If the cake seems to be browning too much before it is cooked, cover it with a layer of tin foil.

Once cooked, remove from the oven and allow to cool for a few minutes before turning out onto a wire rack. Allow to cool fully before icing.

FOR THE ICING

To make the icing, cream the butter and icing sugar together until light and fluffy. Gently stir in the cream cheese until combined, but do not overmix or it may split.

When the cake has cooled, spread the icing over the top and sprinkle with a little more cinnamon before cutting into squares to serve.

BAKER'S TIP

Save the flesh of your carved Halloween pumpkins for this recipe. Remove the seeds, then steam or microwave the flesh until soft.

REFRIGERATOR CAKE

Refrigerator cake is very versatile; you can use any biscuits you like, and it's a great way to use up soft, stale biscuits as they don't need to be crunchy. When it comes to the dried fruit and/or nuts, use any combination you like or need to use up. You can also add things such as popcorn or mini marshmallows if you wish. The trick is to ensure you don't use too much - it all needs to be coated with the chocolate mix in order to set firmly.

Serves: 8
Prep time: 15 minutes, plus 8 hours cooling

280g biscuits (rich tea or ginger nuts work well)
110g butter
170g milk chocolate
1 x 397g tin of condensed milk
50g raisins, glacé cherries, and/or nuts

Grease an 8-inch square or circular tin, or any tin you like - this mixture will not spread, so you can make it as thick or thin as you like.

Crush the biscuits in a food processor or using a rolling pin, leaving some larger chunks if you wish.

Melt the butter and chocolate in a heavy-bottomed pan over a low heat, stirring regularly. Once melted, remove from the heat, add the condensed milk, and stir until well combined.

Add the crushed biscuits and dried fruit and/or nuts, then mix well until fully coated in chocolate.

Press the mixture into the greased tin and pop it in the fridge overnight. Once set, turn it out of the tin and cut into squares.

FOREST FLOOR CUPCAKES

These fun cupcakes are a great addition to an autumn picnic. The meringue mushrooms will keep for several weeks in an airtight container, so you can make them ahead if you like. They even make a lovely snack on their own!

Makes: 12

Prep time: 1 hour 20 minutes, plus 1 hour cooling

Cooking time: 1 hour 20 minutes

Oven temp: Meringues: 100°C fan; Cupcakes: 160°C fan

FOR THE MERINGUE MUSHROOMS

2 egg whites

120g caster sugar

½ tsp cream of tartar

40g dark chocolate

2 tsp cocoa powder

FOR THE CUPCAKES

90g butter, softened

150g caster sugar

2 eggs

130g plain flour

30g cocoa powder

1 tsp bicarbonate of soda

½ tsp baking powder

60ml milk

FOR THE ICING

100g butter, softened

100g icing sugar

30g cocoa powder

2 tbsp milk

2 tbsp pistachios, finely chopped

YOU WILL NEED

Piping bag with a 1cm tip

12 cupcake cases

FOR THE MERINGUE MUSHROOMS

Line a baking tray with baking parchment. In a clean bowl, using an electric whisk, beat the egg whites for 3 to 4 minutes until they form stiff peaks.

Add the sugar, 1 tablespoon at a time, whisking continuously between additions. Rub a little meringue between your fingers to ensure no grains of sugar remain. Once smooth, whisk in the cream of tartar.

Spoon the mixture into a piping bag with a 1cm tip, or, if necessary, cut 1cm off the tip of the bag. Pipe 36 rounds, in varying sizes, and an equal number of 'stalks'. Use a wet finger to flatten any peaks and bake in the oven for 1 hour. The meringues are ready when they peel off the paper easily. Leave to cool completely for 1 hour.

Once the meringues have cooled, melt the chocolate in a heatproof bowl over a pan of simmering water. Remove from the heat and carefully dip each stalk into the chocolate before sticking it to the base of a mushroom 'cap'. Dust the tops with a little cocoa powder and leave in a cool place until ready to decorate your cupcakes.

FOR THE CUPCAKES

Line a muffin tray with 12 cupcake cases. In a mixing bowl, using a handheld mixer or wooden spoon, beat the butter and sugar until it is smooth and creamy. Add the eggs and mix until combined.

Sift in the flour, cocoa powder, bicarbonate of soda and baking powder. Mix everything together, adding the milk a little at a time, until you have a smooth batter. Evenly divide the mixture between the cupcake cases.

Place the tray in the oven and bake for 15 to 20 minutes, or until a cocktail stick poked into the centre of a cake comes out clean. Remove from the oven and place on a wire rack to cool completely.

FOR THE ICING

Beat the butter until very soft, then mix in the icing sugar and cocoa powder. Add the milk, a little at a time, until the icing is soft and spreadable.

Using a teaspoon, evenly spread the chocolate icing over the surface of each cupcake. Add a few mushrooms to the cakes and finish with a sprinkling of finely chopped pistachios.

BAKER'S TIP

Save your egg yolks to make the cherry curd from the Cherry and Almond Viennese Whirls (see page 100).

LAURA'S STICKY TOFFEE TRAYBAKE

Laura, my sister who baked and wrote many of the recipes in this book, says: "This is perfection in a mouthful. It is moist, sticky and scrumptious, and is delicious when warm with a scoop of vanilla ice cream, lashings of custard, or spooned straight from the tin. It is a true crowd pleaser! The flavours develop with time, so it tastes better a day or even two after being made, making it ideal for a dinner party or for when you've returned from a long, crisp walk with ruddy cheeks and chilly fingers. Light the fire, warm the pudding, and all will be well with the world!"

Makes: 12 squares
Prep time: 25 minutes
Cooking time: 20-30 minutes
Oven temp: 160°C fan

FOR THE SPONGE

230g whole medjool dates, pitted and chopped

180ml boiling water

85g salted butter, softened

140g dark or light soft brown sugar

2 eggs

2 tbsp black treacle

1 tsp vanilla extract

180g self-raising flour

1 tsp bicarbonate of soda

100ml milk

FOR THE SAUCE

180g dark muscovado sugar

50g salted butter, cubed

230ml double cream

1 tbsp black treacle

A pinch of salt

1 tsp vanilla extract

Grease and lightly flour a 30x20cm baking tin.

Add the chopped dates to a bowl with the boiling water and leave to soak for 15 minutes.

Meanwhile, in a separate bowl, cream the butter and sugar until light and fluffy using an electric whisk.

Add the eggs one at a time, beating in between for a minute or so, then mix in the treacle and vanilla extract.

Sift the flour and bicarbonate of soda into another bowl, then gently fold in one third of the sifted ingredients before adding half the milk. Repeat until the flour and milk are fully incorporated.

Mash the dates with a fork and stir into the sponge mixture. It will look slightly curdled, but that is okay! Pour the batter into the prepared tray and bake for 20 to 30 minutes until an inserted skewer comes out clean.

Whilst the pudding is baking, prepare the sauce. Add the sugar, butter, and half the cream to a heavy-bottomed pan. Heat over a medium heat, stirring continuously, until the sugar and butter have melted. Add the treacle, salt, and vanilla and bubble for 2 to 3 minutes, stirring continuously. Remove from the heat and stir in the rest of the cream.

When the pudding has baked, remove it from the oven and pour half the sauce over the top. Keep the other half back for when you serve, and leave the pudding in the tray until ready to serve.

LAURA'S TIP

If you make this ahead of time, add any toffee sauce at the time of serving. It can be served as a cake or served warm as pudding.

TOFFEE APPLE LOAF CAKE

A really autumnal cake, but one I wouldn't mind eating any time! It's very moreish with a light, appley cake and a delicious caramel topping.

Serves: 6-8
Prep time: 30 minutes
Cooking time: 55 minutes
Oven temp: 160°C fan

FOR THE CAKE

1 apple, peeled, cored and finely chopped

170g self-raising flour

170g butter, softened

170g caster sugar

3 eggs

½ tsp ground cinnamon

2 tbsp milk

FOR THE TOFFEE SAUCE

30g butter

25g dark soft brown sugar

30ml double cream

A pinch of salt

¼ tsp vanilla extract

FOR THE TOFFEE ICING

40g butter, softened

75g icing sugar

20g toffee sauce (above)

20g pecans, roughly chopped, to decorate

FOR THE CAKE

Grease a loaf tin and lightly dust the base and sides with flour, weighing out any excess flour for the batter.

Place the chopped apple and 1 tablespoon of the flour into a bowl, then toss together so the apple is completely dusted with flour. This will help ensure the apple does not sink in the cake batter during baking.

In a separate bowl, cream together the butter and caster sugar until light and fluffy. Gradually beat in the eggs until combined then stir through the cinnamon and milk. Add the flour and mix until smooth, then fold in the apple until evenly distributed throughout the mixture.

Pour the batter into the prepared cake tin and smooth over the top with the back of a spoon. Bake for 45 minutes, then test the cake by poking a skewer into the centre. If it comes out clean, the cake is baked; if not, return it to the oven for a further 5 minutes and test again. Remove the cake from the oven and leave in the tin to cool completely.

FOR THE TOFFEE SAUCE

Whilst the cake bakes, prepare the toffee sauce. Add the butter to a small pan and melt over a medium heat. Add the brown sugar, double cream and salt and boil for 3 to 4 minutes, stirring continuously. Remove from the heat and stir through the vanilla extract. Leave to cool.

FOR THE TOFFEE ICING

Once the toffee sauce has cooled, prepare the toffee icing. Beat the butter for 1 minute then add the icing sugar and continue to beat until smooth and fluffy. Add 20g of the cooled toffee sauce and mix together until combined.

Remove the cooled cake from the tin, spread the icing over the surface of the cake, then drizzle over the remaining toffee sauce. To finish, roughly chop the pecans and scatter them over the top of the cake. Enjoy!

APPLE SCRAP JELLY

An excellent way of using up waste products, this apple jelly is lovely on a slice of hot buttered toast, alongside cheese, or even stirred through a casserole. It is also adaptable, so why not try adding chilli for a kick of heat, or boiling with a cinnamon stick to add festive flavour? The quantities here are a guide; as you will see, this recipe can be adjusted to the amount of apple scraps you have.

Makes: 3 standard jam jars (370ml each)
Prep time: 30 minutes
Cooking time: 1.5-2 hours

Scraps of 10 apples (peel and cores)
3L water
800g granulated sugar
100ml lemon juice

Add the apple peel and cores to a large saucepan and cover with enough water to make them float.

Bring to a rolling boil and cook until the apple is soft and mushy and the liquid has reduced by half. (This will take about an hour for the quantities given).

Strain the apple scraps using a fine sieve, jam bag, or muslin. If you squeeze the apples, the jelly will be cloudy – this does not impact the flavour, but if you prefer a clear jelly, leave to drain for several hours or overnight using a jam bag or muslin suspended over a bowl. Compost the remaining pulp, if possible.

Next, measure the apple liquid – for every 200ml of liquid, you need 100g sugar and 1 tablespoon of lemon juice. Put a couple of ceramic plates in the freezer to use later to test the setting point.

Bring the apple liquid, sugar, and lemon juice to a boil until it reaches the setting point. Test first after about 15 minutes by reducing the temperature of the jelly (so it does not go past setting point) and putting a teaspoon of it onto one of the cold plates. Put it in the fridge for 1 minute, then push your finger through the jelly. You are looking for the jelly to separate and not run back together and for there to be a thin skin on the top. If it is not ready, boil for another 5 minutes before testing again on the other cold plate. Repeat until the setting point is reached.

Pour the jelly into hot, clean jars - if the jars are fully sterilised, the jelly will keep for a year or more in a cool, dark cupboard. Otherwise, keep for up to a month and refrigerate once opened.

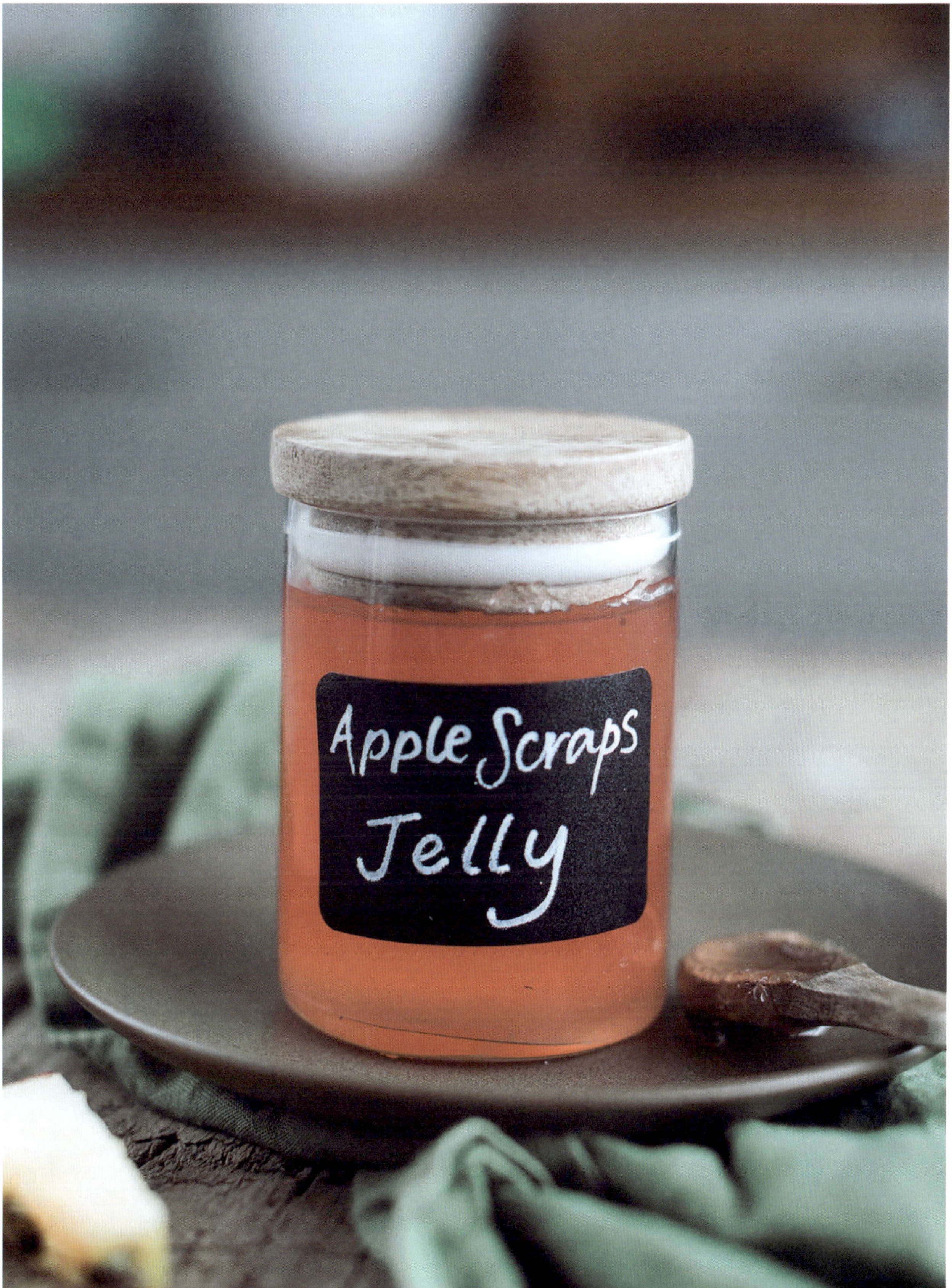
Apple Scraps
Jelly

HOW TO SAVE FOOD MILES, ENERGY AND MONEY

"WHAT YOU DO MAKES A DIFFERENCE,
AND YOU HAVE TO DECIDE WHAT KIND OF
DIFFERENCE YOU WANT TO MAKE."
– DR JANE GOODALL, SCIENTIST AND ACTIVIST

If you are interested in learning more about the carbon footprint of everyday items, then the book *How Bad Are Bananas?* by Mike Berners-Lee is a great place to start. It is an everyday guide and provides easy-to-understand information to help you make more sustainable choices.

GREEN ENERGY

A great way of reducing your carbon footprint is to be on a green energy tariff. This is because when coal, gas and oil are burned they release stored carbon back into the atmosphere, whereas electricity produced from wind, water or solar does not emit carbon.

The energy world is complicated, and it is important to use a provider that invests in renewable energy, rather than one that purchases renewable energy certificates, which are dubious at best. According to The Ethical Consumer, the best options in the UK currently are Ecotricity, Good Energy, and Green Energy UK. This is not to say renewable energy has no negative impact at all, so do turn off your lights, shut down your laptops, and only boil the water you need. Small changes add up and the planet will be grateful!

MICROWAVES

If you have a microwave then use it when something needs warming or melting – butter on a cold, wintery day or chocolate for drizzling can be heated quickly and easily in a microwave using minimal energy.

KNOW YOUR OVEN

Traditionally, recipes have begun with "Preheat your oven", but we have intentionally not done this as most modern ovens will reach temperature in 5 to 10 minutes, so there is no need to turn your oven on until just before you need to bake. By knowing how long your oven will take to heat up, you can read through the recipe and know when you actually need to turn it on.

Some ovens do not bake evenly, so it is worth paying attention so you know if there are hot spots – if there are, you may need to turn your bake half or three-quarters of the way through baking.

DON'T WASTE HEAT

If you're doing a longer bake, you could tuck some jacket potatoes in, or bake more than one thing at a time. The residual heat can also be used to warm something through or to cook a lower temperature bake such as meringues. Opening the oven door makes it lose heat, and it can also cause your bake to sink in the middle, so resist the urge to peek too soon!

LOCAL, CHEMICAL-FREE PRODUCE

The absolute best ingredients for the planet are those that are grown locally and without chemicals: it reduces food miles, and organic soils are about 25% more effective at storing carbon. There are often people who grow too much of the same thing and will happily swap for something else, or for a jar of whatever you make in return. Don't be shy to put yourself out there and ask – trust us when we say there are like-minded people around!

Local does not just have to mean within the couple of miles closest to your home. Think about it as an expanding circle: from your own garden, to local allotments, to the nearest farm shop, to UK-wide. If you aim to bake seasonally and get what you need from as close to home as possible, then you will be having a positive impact for the following reasons:

Freshness: Food will be fresher and have more nutrients. Locally grown fruit (and vegetables) will have less time from harvest to table, meaning it is more nutrient dense than produce that has been grown further away or has made its way through a long supermarket chain.

Fewer food miles, less environmental impact: Local, seasonal food has travelled less distance and therefore, in general, is better for the environment. It can be a tricky balance: for example, choosing non-organic from close to home or organic from further away; if you can get organic and local, you have hit the jackpot!

Taste: It just tastes better. The sweetest fruits are those which are in season. If you have ever plucked a strawberry straight from the plant or a plum from a tree, you will know they just cannot be compared with the bland stuff that is available year-round in the supermarkets.

Local economy: Buying from individuals or small, local shops keeps money flowing in your local economy whilst supporting local farmers and producers. You are able to ask about the food and where it is from, learn about the farming practices in your area, and support those who align with your values. In turn, this helps keep green spaces green and supports biodiversity in your area.

If you shop locally and seasonally and do all you can to prevent food going to landfill, that will hugely impact the carbon footprint of your kitchen!

WINTER

As the days shorten, we naturally move inside, and baking is a homely, comforting thing to do on a Sunday afternoon. Not much fruit is in season, but we can make use of preserves and dried fruit and nuts. Try and choose organic, fairtrade options to support farmers who are doing their bit to help the planet.

When buying fresh fruit, consider food miles; for example, it's better to buy from Morocco than Chile as it's so much closer. A lot of food coming from afar is packaged in plastic, but it's possible to buy dried fruit and nuts from refill shops which are becoming increasingly common, or have refills delivered from online companies such as Abel and Cole.

As winter really sets in, the perfect weekend involves going for a frosty walk to pick sloe berries in cosy jumpers, hats and gloves, and returning for a warming coffee and a slice of sweet, fresh bread by the fire. Try our White Chocolate and Cranberry Babka (page 166) or Cinnamon Roll Wreath (196) for a gathering with friends. Once you've warmed up, weigh out your sloe harvest and make sloe gin by adding half the amount of sugar and double the amount of gin. Store in a bottle in a cool, dark place, shaking every now and then, and enjoy it after at least three months have passed.

As the festive season draws nearer, it's always tempting to bake more and share creations with friends and family, or even make homemade Christmas gifts. A panettone (page 186) or a stack of mince pies (page 182) is always a welcome present, or you could even make a big batch of fudge (page 36) and divide it between your favourite people. Christmas pudding, mincemeat and Christmas cake can all be made months ahead (and taste better as the flavours mature), which'll free up time for wrapping presents as the day draws nearer.

If you find you have dried fruit and nuts to use up, make chocolate bark. Melt your favourite chocolate (white, milk, and dark will all work well) and sprinkle the fruit and nuts on top. Allow to set, then break into shards and gift, or pop in an airtight container for a quick treat.

WHITE CHOCOLATE AND CRANBERRY BABKA

A warming, sweet bake that is an ideal treat for brunch. Served with fresh coffee, of course!

Makes: 1 loaf

Prep time: 30 minutes, plus 1 hour 45 minutes proving

Cooking time: 45 minutes

Oven temp: 180°C fan

FOR THE DOUGH

120ml lukewarm milk

1½ tsp instant yeast

20g caster sugar

260g plain flour

½ tsp salt

1 egg, beaten

80g salted butter, softened

FOR THE FILLING

40g salted butter

80g white chocolate

30g dried cranberries, finely chopped

20g ground almonds

FOR THE GLAZE

20g caster sugar

20ml water

FOR THE TOPPING

Reserved cranberries

Almond flakes

20g white chocolate, chopped

In a jug, mix the warm milk, yeast, and 1 teaspoon of the caster sugar. Set aside for 10 minutes until foamy.

In a large bowl, or the bowl of a stand mixer with a dough hook attached, combine the remaining caster sugar, flour and salt. Add the egg and yeast mixture to the bowl and mix until the dough comes together. Increase the speed to medium and mix for a further 10 minutes, or knead by hand until you have a soft, smooth dough.

Add the softened butter to the dough, a little at a time, ensuring it is fully combined before adding more. If you are working by hand this may take a little longer, but persist, it will come together! Once the butter is incorporated, continue to knead for a further 5 minutes to form a very soft, smooth dough. Transfer the dough to a lightly oiled bowl and cover with a clean, damp tea towel. Leave in a warm place to rise for about an hour.

Meanwhile, make the white chocolate filling. Melt the butter in a small saucepan over a medium heat. Remove from the heat and add the white chocolate, stirring until the chocolate melts. Reserve 1 tablespoon of the dried cranberries for the topping then add the remaining to the chocolate mixture, along with the ground almonds. Mix until combined.

Place the risen dough on a floured surface and roll out into a large rectangle, about 5mm thick, 35cm long, and as wide as possible. Evenly spread the filling over the surface of the dough then, starting at the 35cm edge, roll the dough into a long sausage shape.

Line a round, 8-inch cake tin with baking parchment. Use a sharp knife to cut the dough in half lengthways, then twist the two strips of dough together, with the filling facing upwards, to create a plait-like length of dough. Shape the 'plait' into a round loaf, tucking the ends into the centre, and place in the lined tin. Cover with a clean, damp tea towel and leave to prove for a further 45 minutes or until doubled in size.

Bake the babka for 15 minutes at 180°C fan before reducing to 160°C fan for a final 15 to 20 minutes. If the babka is baking unevenly, rotate the loaf halfway through. If the filling starts to burn, cover loosely with tin foil.

While the loaf is in the oven, make the syrup glaze. Bring the sugar and water to a boil in a small saucepan, and once the sugar has dissolved, remove from heat and set aside to cool. As soon as the bread comes out of the oven, brush the syrup over the surface. Sprinkle over the reserved cranberries and almond flakes and leave to cool slightly for a few minutes. While the bread is still warm, carefully remove it from the tin and place on a wire rack to cool completely.

Once the babka is cool, melt the white chocolate and use a spoon to drizzle it over the surface of the loaf to finish.

FIRESIDE CUPCAKES

These cupcakes are satisfying to assemble and a fun, cosy treat for winter. They're best enjoyed by the warmth of a roaring fire.

Makes: 12
Prep time: 40 minutes
Cooking time: 15-20 minutes
Oven temp: 160°C fan

FOR THE CUPCAKES

90g butter, softened

150g caster sugar

2 eggs

130g plain flour

30g cocoa powder

1 tsp bicarbonate of soda

1 tsp baking powder

60ml milk

FOR THE ICING

100g butter, softened

100g icing sugar

1 tsp vanilla extract

2 tbsp milk

A few drops of yellow food colouring (adjust as needed)

A few drops of orange food colouring (adjust as needed)

TO DECORATE

Yellow sprinkles (optional)

Pretzel sticks

YOU WILL NEED

3 piping bags with a 2cm tip

FOR THE CUPCAKES

Line a muffin tray with 12 cupcake cases. In a mixing bowl, using a handheld mixer or wooden spoon, beat together the butter and sugar until smooth and creamy. Add the eggs and mix together until combined. Sift in the flour, cocoa powder, bicarbonate of soda and baking powder. Mix everything together, adding the milk a little at a time, until you have a smooth batter. Evenly divide the mixture between the cupcake cases.

Transfer the tray in the oven and bake for 15 to 20 minutes, or until a cocktail stick poked into the centre of a cupcake comes out clean. Remove from the oven and place them on a wire rack to cool completely.

FOR THE ICING

Beat the butter until very soft, then add the icing sugar and vanilla and mix together. Add the milk, a little at a time, until the icing is soft and smooth.

Divide the icing equally between two small bowls. Add yellow food colouring to the first bowl, mixing until fully combined. Spoon the icing into a piping bag. Repeat the process with the second bowl and the orange food colouring.

Place both the yellow and orange piping bags inside the third piping bag and tie a knot in the opening, this will enable you to pipe both colours at the same time!

If necessary, use a pair of scissors to snip 2cm from the tip of the piping bags, then pipe each cupcake in a swirling motion to create the orange and yellow flames.

Add some sprinkles, if using, to each cupcake, then finish with a few pretzel 'logs' to finish your fire.

BAKER'S TIP

You can make these cupcakes in autumn too as they're a great way to celebrate Bonfire Night!

EMILY'S BOOZY COFFEE CUPCAKES

Emily, my sister-in-law, says: "These light, tiramisu-style cupcakes were a hit at my brother's wedding and have since become a must at every family gathering. With the perfect balance of coffee and creamy flavours, they're indulgent without being overly sweet – so good it's hard to stop at just one!"

Makes: 12
Prep time: 25 minutes
Cooking time: 20-25 minutes
Oven temp: 180°C fan

FOR THE CUPCAKES
220g plain flour
200g caster sugar
1 tsp bicarbonate of soda
200ml milk
2 tsp vanilla extract
80ml vegetable oil
1 tsp red or white wine vinegar
40ml espresso or strong instant coffee, cooled (for the latter, about 3 tsp coffee mixed with 40ml water)

FOR THE ICING
110g butter
260g icing sugar
1 tsp vanilla extract
40ml espresso martini or coffee liqueur

TO DECORATE
Coffee beans
Cocoa powder, for dusting

Line a muffin tray with 12 cupcake cases. Mix the flour in a bowl with the sugar and bicarbonate of soda. Add the milk, vanilla extract, vegetable oil, vinegar, and coffee and fold until just combined. The batter will be runny, so it's easiest to transfer it to a jug and pour it into the cupcake cases. Make sure they all have an equal amount of cake mix, then bake for 20 to 25 minutes. Check the cakes after 20 minutes, and if a cocktail stick inserted into the centre doesn't come out clean, put them back in for 5 more minutes.

Make the icing by adding the butter, icing sugar, vanilla extract, and coffee liqueur to a bowl. Mix with an electric whisk until smooth, then pipe or spoon onto each cupcake. Finish with a few coffee beans and a dusting of cocoa powder.

EMILY'S TIP
If you don't have any boozy coffee for the icing, you can just use espresso or strong instant coffee – or add a little Marsala wine for an extra kick.

For crowd pleasing vegan cupcakes, use plant-based milk and a vegan butter block.

CHOCOLATE FUDGE CAKE

This moreish take on a brownie should be a staple in every chocolate lover's kitchen. It is gooey in the middle and firm yet chewy on the edges – perfect for picnics or a coffee stop on a long, chilly walk.

Makes: 12
Prep time: 20 minutes
Cooking time: 40 minutes
Oven temp: 160°C fan

170g butter
425g caster sugar
3 eggs
255g plain flour
85g cocoa powder
1 tsp vanilla extract

Grease a 20x25cm baking tin and dust the sides and base with cocoa powder.

In a heavy-bottomed saucepan, melt the butter over a medium heat. Once melted, add the sugar and eggs and beat together with a wooden spoon.

Add the flour, cocoa powder, and vanilla extract and mix well. It will be thick and sticky, so you'll need some elbow grease to fully combine it!

Pour the mixture into the prepared tin and spread it out evenly. Bake for 40 minutes – it will be cooked when the edges are firm and the centre has the slightest wobble when the tin is lightly shaken.

Leave to cool in the tin before turning out and cutting into squares.

GINGERBREAD DOUGHNUTS

These doughnuts take a little bit of extra effort to make, but NOTHING beats the taste and satisfaction of a fresh, homemade doughnut. The warming gingerbread custard elevates these ones to another level.

Makes: 8-9
Prep time: 2 hours 20 minutes, plus 1 hour 25 proving
Cooking time: 25 minutes

FOR THE FILLING

50g egg yolk (approx. 3 medium egg yolks)

50g light soft brown sugar

15g cornflour

200ml milk

¾ tsp ground cinnamon

1 ¼ tsp mixed spice

¼ tsp ground ginger

10g room temperature butter

150g whipping cream

FOR THE DOUGHNUTS

1 tsp yeast

120ml lukewarm milk

1 ½ tbsp light soft brown sugar

280g plain flour

½ tsp salt

1 tsp ground cinnamon

3 tsp ground ginger

1 egg

1 tbsp golden syrup

45g butter, softened

50g granulated sugar

750ml sunflower oil, for frying

YOU WILL NEED

6cm circular cutter

A piping bag with a 1cm tip

FOR THE FILLING

Whisk the egg yolk, sugar, and cornflour together in a large bowl. In a small pan, gently warm the milk and spices. Remove from the heat, add half to the egg yolk mixture, and whisk briskly for 30 seconds before adding the remaining half. Return the mixture to the pan and whisk over a medium heat until very thick.

Remove from the heat, add the butter, and stir to combine. Leave to stand for 10 minutes, whisking occasionally, then transfer to a bowl to cool. Place cling film across the cream's surface to prevent a skin forming, then refrigerate.

Once chilled, whisk the whipping cream until it forms stiff peaks, then gently fold it into the pastry cream. Refrigerate until ready to use.

FOR THE DOUGHNUTS

Combine the yeast, milk, and half of the brown sugar in a jug. Leave to stand for about 10 minutes, until foamy.

In a large bowl, or stand mixer with a dough hook, combine the flour, salt, spices, and remaining brown sugar. Add the yeast mixture, egg, and syrup and mix until it forms a dough. Knead until soft and smooth.

Add the softened butter, little by little, to the dough, ensuring it's fully combined before adding more. Once incorporated, knead for 5 minutes until very soft and smooth. Transfer to a lightly oiled bowl, cover with a clean, damp tea towel, and leave in a warm place to prove for an hour.

Turn the dough out onto a floured surface and roll out to about 2cm thick. Leave to rest for 5 minutes. Using a 6cm circular cutter, or the rim of a glass, cut out as many doughnuts as possible. Place them on a lined baking tray, then cover with a clean, damp tea towel to prove for another 20 minutes.

Tip the granulated sugar into a bowl and set aside. Then, heat the oil in a large pan to about 175°C. Use a scrap of dough to test the oil: if it floats, gently bubbles at the edges, and turns golden brown after a minute or so, it's ready.

Lower the doughnuts into the pan using a slotted spoon. Cook in batches of two for 1 and half to 2 minutes each side, or until golden brown. Transfer to a wire rack for about 30 seconds before tossing in the sugar, then repeat with the remaining doughnuts.

Once cooled, poke a hole in each doughnut, opening it up slightly for the filling. Scoop the cream filling into a piping bag and snip about 1cm off the tip. Fill each doughnut with cream and enjoy!

BAKER'S TIP

These are best enjoyed the same day but will keep in the fridge in an airtight container. You can also save your egg whites to make meringues.

COFFEE, RYE, AND CHOCOLATE CHIP COOKIES

These grown-up cookies have a deep flavour, and the coffee usually means you can enjoy them without the children trying to steal one! Check out the Baker's Tip for a vegan-friendly version.

Makes: 20 cookies
Prep time: 1 hour, plus 2 hours chilling
Cooking time: 10-12 minutes
Oven temp: 160°C fan

110g unsalted butter
1½ tbsp ground coffee
100g self-raising flour
110g wholemeal rye flour
¼ tsp salt
100g light soft brown sugar
75g caster sugar
1 egg
1 tbsp milk
½ tsp vanilla extract
150g dark chocolate chips
½ tsp flaky sea salt

Melt the butter in a small pan over a medium heat until it just starts to bubble. Remove from the heat and stir through the ground coffee, then set aside to cool slightly.

Sift the self-raising flour, rye flour, and salt into a small bowl. Then, in a separate bowl, combine the coffee butter, sugars, egg, milk and vanilla extract. Add the sifted ingredients and stir until well combined.

Add the chocolate chips and mix until evenly distributed throughout the dough. Cover the bowl and refrigerate for at least 2 hours, or overnight if you can wait that long!

Line two baking trays with reusable silicone sheets or baking parchment. Scoop a tablespoon of mixture for each cookie onto the prepared baking trays, leaving space between each one to allow for spreading. You may need to bake these in batches, depending on the size of your baking trays.

Sprinkle a little flaky sea salt on top of each cookie and bake for 10 to 12 minutes until golden at the edges.

Remove from the oven and leave to cool completely on the baking tray. Enjoy with your favourite cup of coffee.

BAKER'S TIP
These cookies are equally delicious if you opt for vegan alternatives. For a vegan version, we use plant-based butter, oat milk, and half a mashed banana to replace the egg. You should also ensure your chocolate is dairy-free.

LUCY'S CHOCOLATE TORTE

Lucy, my sister, says: "Very rich and decadent, this torte needs a sharp coulis to cut through and elevate the chocolate flavour. If you need a gluten-free version, you can leave out the flour; the torte will be very soft but equally delicious."

Serves 12
Prep time: 25 minutes
Cooking time: 50 minutes
Oven temp: 130°C fan

FOR THE TORTE

1 tbsp cocoa powder, for dusting

350g dark chocolate (80% cocoa solids)

225g salted butter

5 eggs

250g caster sugar

1 tbsp plain flour

FOR THE COULIS

500g frozen raspberries

1 tbsp icing sugar

½ lemon, juiced

FOR THE TORTE

Grease a 9-inch cake tin and dust the base and sides with cocoa powder (do not use a springform tin as they're not watertight and this will stand in water to bake!).

Melt the chocolate and butter together in a microwave or over a pan of simmering water. Once melted, leave to stand for a few minutes.

Meanwhile, whisk the eggs and sugar together in a separate bowl until light, fluffy, and tripled in size. Tip the melted chocolate and flour into the egg-sugar mixture and whisk to combine before pouring into the prepared tin.

To bake, transfer the tin to a large, deep baking tray and fill the baking tray with boiling water so that it comes about halfway up the sides of the cake tin. Bake for 50 minutes until there is a slight wobble in the centre of the torte when tapped.

Remove from the oven and leave to cool in the water-filled baking tray for at least an hour before turning out onto a board or serving platter.

FOR THE COULIS

Add all the ingredients to a saucepan over a medium heat and warm through, stirring until the raspberries have broken down and the sugar has dissolved. If you prefer a completely smooth coulis, pass the mixture through a fine sieve and compost the raspberry seeds.

To serve, dust the torte with icing sugar and serve with a generous drizzle of the raspberry coulis.

CLARE'S MINCEMEAT

Clare, the head baker at Honeywell Bakes, says: "This is a recipe that my mum found many years ago (we think from a Farmers Weekly), and it is used every year because our family don't like mixed peel, making this ideal as there are no hard lumps in it!"

Makes: 3 large jars (approx. 1.4kg)
Prep time: 20 minutes

225g suet
225g currants
1 lemon, zested
110g demerara sugar
225g sultanas
225g raisins
225g cooking apples, peeled and sliced
2 tbsp brandy

Clean the jars and lids by soaking them in very hot, soapy water. If you are planning on keeping the mincemeat for more than a few weeks, or out of the fridge, sterilise the jars properly using an oven.

Place the suet, currants, lemon zest and sugar in a large bowl and mix well. Mince together the sultanas, raisins and cooking apples. You can do this with a mincer or food processor. For a chunkier mincemeat, roughly chop the ingredients by hand.

Mix all the ingredients together thoroughly, then add the brandy and stir well. Pack the mincemeat into the jars and seal tightly. It will last for several weeks in the fridge, or if fully sterilised will last for months unopened.

CLARE'S TIP

Once made, store the mincemeat in a cool, dark place, and when ready to use, stir in an extra tablespoon of brandy and mix well! This can be made well ahead of time, and I always make mine at the end of October. It will also work with mixed peel if you like it!

FRANGIPANE MINCE PIES

A slightly different take on a traditional mince pie, these can be decorated with pastry stars or just dusted with icing sugar. We like to serve them warm with a mug of mulled wine.

Makes: 12
Prep time: 20 minutes
Cooking time: 30 minutes
Oven temp: 160°C fan

Clare's Mincemeat (see page 180)

FOR THE PASTRY
240g cold butter, cubed
390g plain flour
120g caster sugar

FOR THE FRANGIPANE
60g ground almonds
60g caster sugar
90g plain flour
60g butter, softened
6 tsp milk

TO SERVE
Icing sugar, for dusting

Rub the butter and flour together using your fingertips until it resembles breadcrumbs. Bring the mixture together into a ball, then flatten the ball into a disc, cover in reusable food wrap, and refrigerate for 30 minutes. Meanwhile, lightly grease a muffin tray with a little butter.

Roll the pastry out on a floured surface to 3-5mm thick. Cut out circles (about 10cm) and place the pastry circles in the muffin tray. Don't worry if the pastry tears, just patch it up with any off-cuts. Prick the bases with a fork and bake for 15 minutes. You can roll out any remaining pastry and cut out star shapes, if desired – set them aside to decorate later.

Meanwhile, prepare the frangipane. Combine the dry ingredients then beat in the softened butter and milk until smooth. Spoon a teaspoon of mincemeat into each baked mince pie base, then top with the frangipane mixture and a pastry star. Bake for another 15 minutes until golden. Allow to cool and dust with icing sugar before serving.

GINGERBREAD HOUSE

A gingerbread house is a traditional bake that many people love making. We love to take our time, make some mulled wine, and make a day out of it, often planning our decorations weeks ahead. We also make gingerbread houses for other seasons: a haunted house for Halloween, or a beach house in summer.

Makes: 1 house
Prep time: 2 hours, plus 1 hour chilling
Cooking time: 15-20 minutes
Oven temp: 160°C fan

FOR THE GINGERBREAD

125g salted butter, softened

125g caster sugar

1 medium egg

3 tbsp golden syrup

350g plain flour

100g self-raising flour

2 tsp ground ginger

1 tsp mixed spice

FOR THE ROYAL ICING

150g icing sugar

1 egg white

TO DECORATE

Festive sugar decorations (optional)

Snowflake sprinkles (optional)

Icing sugar, for dusting

YOU WILL NEED

Gingerbread house templates

A piping bag with a small tip, approx 2mm

FOR THE GINGERBREAD

Cut out the gingerbread house templates and set aside for later. For the biscuit dough, beat together the butter and sugar until creamy. Add the egg and golden syrup and mix until combined. Add the plain flour, self-raising flour and spices to the bowl and use your hands to bring the ingredients together to form a dough, kneading until well combined. Chill the dough, wrapped in reusable food wrap or placed in a covered bowl, for 30 minutes.

Once chilled, roll the dough out on a floured surface to approximately 5mm thick. Try to ensure it's evenly rolled so the biscuits bake uniformly. Using a sharp knife or a pizza cutter, cut around the templates. If you would like a more challenging gingerbread house, add windows and doors to your templates. Slide the pieces onto a baking tray lined with a reusable silicone sheet or baking parchment. Place the dough on the tray in the fridge to chill again for 30 minutes; this will help prevent the shapes spreading while they bake.

Bake the gingerbread biscuits for 15 to 20 minutes, or until golden. Turn the tray after the first 10 minutes so the biscuits bake evenly. Remove from the oven and place the biscuits on a wire rack to cool.

FOR THE ROYAL ICING

Add the icing sugar to a bowl with the egg white and mix slowly until you have a thick icing, the consistency of toothpaste. Add a few drops of water at a time if it is too thick, but be careful to add the water slowly as it could quickly become too runny. Spoon the royal icing into a piping bag and snip 2mm off the tip of the bag, or use a piping tip about 2mm in diameter.

TO DECORATE

Decorate the gingerbread panels individually before assembling. Pipe icing along the top and edges of the roof to look like snow and icicles and pipe some windows and doors. Use the icing to stick on the sugar decorations and snowflake sprinkles, if using. Be as creative as you like! Let the icing set for about an hour so it doesn't get damaged when you assemble the house.

To assemble the gingerbread house, pipe some icing along the edges of the panels and stick the biscuits together on a cake board or plate/cake stand. Assemble the sides and gables of the house first, using a tin to prop them up if necessary. Add the roof last and hold it in place for a few minutes until secure.

Fill in any gaps with the remaining royal icing, such as the pitch of the roof, and add some finishing touches. Finally, dust icing sugar around the base of the house, covering the cake board or plate, to look like snow.

BAKER'S TIP

It's really important to chill your dough so that the pieces of your house don't spread during baking. Make sure the royal icing you use as 'glue' is very thick. You can also make some of the icing slightly runnier to decorate your house. Once you've used the template, you can use it to practise your designs by sketching or piping onto the template paper before you decorate your house.

Scan for template

ORANGE AND CRANBERRY PANETTONE

A classic winter bake, these panettones make lovely homemade gifts for friends and family. The recipe will double easily if you want to make extra to give away.

Makes: 4
Prep time: 1 hour 15 minutes, plus 2 hours 30 minutes proving
Cooking time: 25-35 minutes
Oven temp: 130°C fan

FOR THE DOUGH

65g butter, softened

1 egg, beaten

250g strong white bread flour

¼ tsp salt

80ml warm whole milk

65g caster sugar

1 tsp instant yeast

50g dried cranberries

1 orange, zested

TO FINISH

1 egg, beaten

1 tbsp sugar pearls or demerara sugar

YOU WILL NEED

4 tins (standard 400g size, emptied and cleaned)

Unshakable festive cheer

Lightly grease the insides of the tin cans and line each one with a piece of baking parchment, ensuring it is 3cm higher than the top edge of each tin.

In a large bowl, cream together the softened butter and beaten egg until soft and pale. Sift the flour and salt into the mixture and stir together.

In a separate bowl or jug, heat the milk and sugar until just warm to the touch then add the yeast - it is important to ensure the milk isn't too hot as this can kill the yeast.

Gradually add the milk mixture into the large bowl until fully incorporated to form a dough. Sprinkle a little flour onto a clean surface and knead the dough until soft and elastic. This could take up to 10 minutes. If the dough is too wet at this stage, you can add more flour; if too dry, add a little more milk.

Return the dough to the large bowl and cover with a damp tea towel. Leave in a warm place to rise for 1 hour or until doubled in size.

Turn the dough out onto a floured surface, punch it lightly with your fists to knock a little air out, then knead for another 10 minutes. Place the dough into a clean, lightly oiled bowl, cover, and return to a warm place to rise again.

After approximately 1 hour, once the dough has doubled in size again, turn it out onto a floured surface and punch lightly again before sprinkling over the cranberries and orange zest. Knead again to incorporate the cranberries.

Split the dough into four equal portions and place one into each tin can. Cover again and leave to rise one final time for about 30 minutes. When the dough has doubled in size, brush with beaten egg and sprinkle on some sugar pearl nibs or demerara sugar before baking for 25 to 35 minutes, or until a skewer inserted into the centre comes out clean.

Once cooled, carefully remove from the tins and, using your festive cheer, wrap decoratively with paper and twine.

ORANGE CHRISTMAS PUDDING

This Christmas pudding is a lighter version of the traditional one, and the nuts and oranges add extra dimension. You can of course change the nuts and alcohol to others to suit your preference.

Serves: 8
Prep time: 45 minutes plus overnight soaking
Cooking time: 6-8 hours
Oven temp: 140°C fan

350g mixed dried fruit

200g glacé cherries, 100g halved; 100g whole (we use morello)

1 orange, zested and segmented

1 lemon, zested and juiced

120g dark muscovado sugar

2 tsp mixed spice

100ml brandy

50ml almond or hazelnut liqueur

75g blanched almonds

75g pecan nuts

2 eggs, beaten

100g self-raising flour

180g fresh white breadcrumbs

100g butter, frozen

25g butter, softened

2 heaped tbsp golden syrup

Add the mixed fruit, 100g of halved glacé cherries, orange zest, and lemon zest and juice to a bowl with the sugar and mixed spice. Pour in the brandy and liqueur and stir well. Cover and leave to soak overnight.

The next day, grease a 1.5L pudding basin and place a disc of baking parchment in the base. Roughly chop half the almonds and half the pecans, leaving the rest whole.

Combine the eggs, soaked fruit, chopped nuts, flour and breadcrumbs before grating in the frozen butter a little at a time, mixing periodically so the butter disperses evenly throughout the mixture.

In a small bowl, mix the softened butter and golden syrup together before spreading it over the base of the pudding basin and a little up the sides. Scatter the whole nuts, remaining cherries, and orange segments in the base and up the sides of the bowl – think about how you would like it to look when you turn it out as the nuts and fruit can make a lovely pattern!

Spoon the pudding mixture into the basin and level the top. Cover with baking parchment and the lid (if there is one) or a layer of foil. If using foil, use string or a large rubber band to secure it tightly in place.

To bake, place the pudding basin in a deep roasting tin and fill the tin two-thirds deep with hot water. Use foil to create a tent over the pudding and bake for 6 to 8 hours – the longer the baking time, the darker the pudding. Once cooked to your liking, remove and allow to cool fully before storing in the fridge for up to one month.

To reheat for serving, either repeat the oven process for 2 hours, or steam in a large pan with an upturned saucer on the base for 2 hours, then turn out and decorate with holly if desired.

BAKER'S TIP

If you want to keep the pudding (in the fridge) for more than a month, omit the orange segments. It will keep for several months without the orange (we have kept Christmas puddings for up to a year!).

CARDAMOM AND ORANGE SNOWFLAKE BISCUITS

Nothing says Christmas like a homemade iced biscuit! Get creative and have fun piping festive patterns and shapes.

Makes: About 20 biscuits
Prep time: 1 hour, plus overnight chilling
Cooking time: 5-10 minutes, depending on size
Oven temp: 180°C fan

FOR THE BISCUITS

140g plain flour

¼ tsp baking powder

¼ tsp ground ginger

¼ tsp ground cloves

½ tsp ground cinnamon

¼ tsp ground cardamom

40g salted butter, softened

½ orange, zested

50g golden syrup

25g caster sugar

25g dark soft brown sugar

40ml double cream

FOR THE ROYAL ICING

200g icing sugar

1 egg white, or 30g aquafaba (water from a tin of chickpeas)

A little water

YOU WILL NEED

A piping bag with a very small tip

A cookie cutter – we use snowflakes, but be creative! (If you don't have cutters, you could use a jar and a knife to cut out circles, or use a template)

Sift the flour, baking powder and spices into a large mixing bowl and stir to combine. Add the butter, orange zest, golden syrup, caster sugar, brown sugar and double cream. Mix together until well combined, but don't worry if the dough is still quite sticky.

Shape the dough into a log and wrap in reusable food wrap. Refrigerate for several hours, or overnight if possible – the longer, the better!

Line a baking tray with baking parchment. Roll the dough out on a lightly floured surface to the thickness of a £1 coin. Cut out as many snowflake shapes as you can and arrange them on the prepared baking tray.

Bake in the oven for 5 to 6 minutes or until the biscuits have turned a deeper shade of brown. Remove the baked biscuits from the oven and leave to cool on a wire rack.

While the biscuits cool, sift the icing sugar into a bowl with the egg white or aquafaba. Whisk until smooth and the consistency of toothpaste, adding a touch of water if needed.

Transfer the royal icing into a piping bag with a small piping tip attached, if you have one. If necessary, snip off the tip of the piping bag – no more than 1mm.

Pipe festive patterns over the biscuits. You could practise the designs first by placing some baking parchment over a template or piece of card and tracing them with your piping bag.

BAKER'S TIP

If you prefer a gingerbread biscuit, leave out the orange and cardamom and add an extra quarter of a teaspoon of ginger.

Scan for template

CLARE'S CHRISTMAS CAKE

Clare, the head baker at Honeywell Bakes, says: "This Christmas cake recipe has been handed down through our family from my granny; she never shared the recipe with anyone as she liked to think the pineapple was a secret ingredient, but I'm sharing it with all of you. It keeps the cake really nice and moist."

Makes: 1 cake, serves 20
Prep time: 20 minutes, plus 45 minutes to decorate
Cooking time: 2 hours 30 minutes
Oven temp: 130°C fan

FOR THE CAKE

225g salted butter

225g light or dark soft brown sugar

1 orange, zested

1 tbsp black treacle

5 eggs

140g plain flour

450g mixed fruit

55g ground almonds

55g glacé cherries

1 x 227g tin of crushed pineapple, drained (see Clare's Tip)

FOR THE DECORATION (OPTIONAL)

400g marzipan (see Dad's Stollen recipe on page 194)

150g royal icing (see our Gingerbread House recipe on page 184)

2 tbsp apricot jam

A few sprigs of rosemary

Pomegranate seeds

Icing sugar, for dusting

FOR THE CAKE

Grease and flour a deep 8-inch cake tin. In a large bowl, use an electric whisk to cream together the butter, sugar and orange zest. Add the treacle, eggs and flour slowly, mixing as you go. Add all the remaining ingredients and mix well.

Pour the mixture into the prepared tin and bake for 2 and a half hours or until a skewer inserted into the centre comes out clean.

Remove from the oven and allow to cool in the tin for 30 minutes before removing and cooling fully on a wire rack.

FOR THE DECORATION

Decoration is optional and depends on personal preference. If decorating, roll out the marzipan into a rectangle approximately 3mm thick then cut out an 8-inch disc (you can use the cake tin as a template). Re-roll the marzipan and cut it so it's the right length and height of the cake – a piece of string can be a handy measuring tool for the cake's circumference.

Brush the cake on the top and sides with the apricot jam, then place the marzipan disc on top and wrap the sides. Use your hands to smooth and blend any cracks and mould the top into the sides.

Using a palette knife, spread the royal icing all over the cake to create snowy peaks. Poke some sprigs of rosemary into the icing and sprinkle with pomegranate seeds before dusting with icing sugar for a snowy effect.

CLARE'S TIP

Crushed pineapple is sometimes difficult to find, but you can use sliced or diced pineapple, either blended or crushed with a fork.

DAD'S STOLLEN

When I was growing up, Dad didn't bake much, but in recent years he's perfected the art of bread making, and now very rarely buys any bread for the household. There's usually a queue of siblings lining up for his sourdough! This stollen is delicious, with just the right amount of sweetness. It's not just for Christmas – this is a bake we enjoy year-round.

Makes: 1 loaf
Prep time: 30 minutes, plus 3 hours proving
Cooking time: 15-20 minutes
Oven temp: 200°C fan

FOR THE DOUGH

250g strong white bread flour

1 tsp instant yeast

1 tbsp sugar

1 tbsp milk powder (optional)

25g butter, softened

1 medium egg

100ml water

½ tsp salt

125g dried fruit and/or nuts of your choice

FOR THE MARZIPAN

40g golden caster sugar

70g icing sugar

110g ground almonds

1 egg white, 1 egg yolk, or 30g water

Few drops of almond essence (optional)

FOR THE TOPPING

10g butter, melted

1 tbsp icing sugar, for dusting

Mix the flour, yeast, sugar, and milk powder together in a bowl with a spoon or stand mixer, if you have one. Add the butter, egg, water, and salt and mix until a dough forms. Knead for 10 minutes, then cover with a clean, damp tea towel and leave to rise in a warm place for an hour.

Knead in the dried fruit and nuts; apricots, cherries, raisins, mixed peel, chopped hazelnuts, brazils or pecans all work well – use your faves! Allow to rise for another hour in the bowl, again covered in a damp tea towel, until doubled in size.

Whilst the dough proves, make the marzipan. Mix the sugars and ground almonds in a bowl, then make a well in the middle and add the egg or water and almond essence, if using. Mix together until a dough forms.

Dust a work surface with icing sugar, then knead the marzipan briefly until it forms a smooth ball, adding a bit more icing sugar if it seems too wet. Cover and set aside until ready to use.

Turn the dough out onto a floured worktop and roll it out into an oval. Roll the marzipan into a long sausage and place it on top of the dough lengthwise, about a third of the way in. Fold the dough over the marzipan, gently pressing the edges together, and place the stollen onto a lined baking tray. Cover with a tea towel and leave to rise for one final hour.

Once risen, bake for 15 to 20 minutes until golden. While still warm, brush melted butter over the top and dust liberally with icing sugar.

DAD'S TIP

You can use a bread machine to mix the dough if it has a nut dispenser – use a raisin bread dough programme then turn the dough out onto a floured worktop after the second prove and follow the recipe from there.

I often double the quantities if we have a big gathering, and if time is short, I just buy the marzipan!

CINNAMON ROLL WREATH

A stunning centrepiece, this wreath is best shared with family or friends, and we've often made it for brunch on Christmas day. You can do the second prove in the fridge overnight, just bring it to room temperature before baking. The smell of warm cinnamon rolls baking is as festive as it comes!

Serves: 8
Prep time: 50 minutes, plus 2 hours proving
Cooking time: 15-20 minutes
Oven temp: 180°C fan

FOR THE DOUGH

145ml warm milk

1½ tsp instant yeast

40g caster sugar

340g strong white bread flour

1 egg, plus 1 egg yolk

40g salted butter, melted

FOR THE FILLING

100g light soft brown sugar

1 tbsp ground cinnamon

1 tsp ground ginger

1 orange, zested

50g dried cranberries (optional)

40g salted butter, softened

FOR THE ICING

40g salted butter, softened

75g icing sugar

75g full-fat cream cheese

½ tbsp fresh orange juice

FOR THE TOPPING (OPTIONAL)

1 tbsp pistachios, chopped

1 tbsp dried cranberries

To make the dough, start by mixing the warm milk, yeast and 1 teaspoon of caster sugar in a jug. Leave to stand for about 10 minutes until foamy.

In a large bowl, or the bowl of a stand mixer with a dough hook attached, combine the flour and remaining caster sugar. Add the egg, egg yolk, melted butter and yeast mixture to the bowl and mix until the dough comes together. Increase the speed to medium and mix for a further 10 minutes, or knead by hand until you have soft, smooth dough. Transfer the dough to a lightly oiled bowl and cover with a clean, damp tea towel. Leave in a warm place to rise for about 1 hour.

Meanwhile, prepare the filling. Stir together the brown sugar, cinnamon, ginger and orange zest. Roughly chop the cranberries, if using, and add to the mixture. Set aside for later.

Once risen, turn the dough out onto a floured surface and roll out into a large rectangle, about 1cm thick, then loosely cover with a clean, damp tea towel and leave to rest for 5 minutes. Spread the softened butter over the surface of the dough, leaving a gap of about 1cm along one of the long edges. Evenly sprinkle the spiced cranberry mixture over the buttered dough, carefully rubbing it into the butter.

Line a large baking tray with a reusable silicone sheet or baking parchment. Starting at the long edge without the border, carefully roll up the dough. Trim about 2cm off each end, removing any dough that doesn't have much filling (you can bake these separately and eat them!). Arrange the roll in a circle, seam side down, on the prepared baking tray.

Using a sharp knife, cut the dough circle into 24 rolls, slicing three-quarters of the way through so they are still connected in the middle. To shape the wreath, turn one of the cinnamon rolls at the end on its side. Turn the next one so that it slightly overlaps the first, then repeat with each roll, forming a circle and overlapping as you go.

Loosely cover the wreath with a clean, damp tea towel and leave in a warm place to rise for 1 hour, or until risen and puffy. Uncover the wreath, place in the centre of the oven, and bake for 15 to 20 minutes or until lightly golden. Remove from the oven and leave to cool for 15 minutes before icing.

Whilst the wreath cools, prepare the cream cheese icing. In a mixing bowl, beat together the softened butter and icing sugar until light and fluffy. Fold through the cream cheese, being careful not to overwork the mixture or it will become too runny. Add the freshly squeezed orange juice and mix briefly.

Drizzle the icing over the wreath, then finish with a scattering of chopped pistachios and cranberries.

BAKER'S TIP

You can make these into 'normal' cinnamon rolls by cutting them into slices instead of forming them into a wreath.

POVITICA

Povitica (pronounced pov-e-tee-za) is an Eastern European bread enjoyed over the Christmas period. The texture is similar to brioche and the dough is swirled around a cinnamon and walnut filling.

Makes: 1 loaf
Prep time: 1 hour, plus 2 hours proving
Cooking time: 45 minutes
Oven temp: 160°C fan

FOR THE DOUGH

25g caster sugar

1 ½ tsp instant yeast

80ml lukewarm milk

200g plain flour

¼ tsp fine sea salt

20g salted butter, melted

30g beaten egg (reserve any remainder for the glaze)

¼ tsp vanilla extract

FOR THE FILLING

20g salted butter

2 tbsp milk

50g walnuts

50g caster sugar

2 tbsp cocoa powder

¼ tsp ground cinnamon

½ tsp vanilla extract

TO ASSEMBLE

Reserved egg, for the glaze

10g butter, melted

1 tbsp icing sugar

In a jug, mix 1 teaspoon of the caster sugar with the instant yeast and warm milk. Set aside for 10 minutes until foamy.

Meanwhile, in a large mixing bowl or the bowl of a stand mixer with a dough hook attachment, stir together the flour, salt and remaining sugar. Make a well in the centre and add the yeast mixture, melted butter, beaten egg, and vanilla extract. If using a mixer, knead for 8 to 10 minutes; if kneading by hand, do so on a floured surface for 10 to 15 minutes until soft, smooth and stretchy.

Place the dough in a lightly oiled bowl, cover with a clean, damp tea towel or clean shower cap and leave to rise for 1 hour, or until doubled in size. Grease a 1lb loaf tin and set aside.

While the dough is proving, prepare the filling. Combine the butter and milk in a small pan and heat gently until the butter has melted. Remove from the heat and set aside. Add the walnuts, sugar, cocoa powder and cinnamon to a food processor and blend until grainy. Add the vanilla extract and milk and butter mixture and pulse to combine. Set aside.

To assemble, turn the dough out onto a floured surface and divide it in half. Carefully roll the first portion out into a large rectangle. Dust your hands with flour and ease them underneath the dough. Using your hands, stretch the dough out from the centre until very thin and almost see-through. The rectangle should be twice the length of your loaf tin.

Brush the surface of the dough with melted butter and spread over half of the walnut filling, taking care not to tear the dough. If the paste is too thick and sticky, add a little warm milk to loosen it.

Starting at the long edge of the dough, gently roll the dough up tightly, like a Swiss roll. Repeat the whole process with the second portion.

Carefully lift the first dough roll into the prepared loaf tin, arranging it in a 'U' shape in the bottom of the tin. Place the second roll on top, so that the 'U' is going in the opposite direction. Cover the tin with a damp tea towel and leave to prove for 1 hour.

Once risen, brush the surface of the dough with the reserved beaten egg and bake for 15 minutes at 160°C fan. Reduce the temperature to 130°C fan and bake for a further 30 to 35 minutes or until a rich golden-brown.

Remove from the oven and leave to cool before removing from the tin. Brushed with the melted butter and dust with icing sugar before serving.

BLACK FOREST YULE LOG

This bake takes a bit of time, but it looks amazing. If you're in a hurry, decorate with sprigs of holly instead of the meringue mushrooms.

Makes: 1 log, serves 6-8
Prep time: 4 hours
Cooking time: 1 hour 15 minutes
Oven temp: Meringues: 100°C fan;
Cake: 160°C fan

FOR THE MERINGUE MUSHROOMS

1 egg white

60g caster sugar

A pinch of cream of tartar

20g dark chocolate

1 tsp cocoa powder

FOR THE CREAM FILLING

250ml double cream

30g icing sugar

15g dried cherries or cranberries

FOR THE CHOCOLATE GANACHE

80ml double cream

100g dark chocolate

Icing sugar, for dusting

FOR THE CHOCOLATE SPONGE

Butter, for greasing

4 eggs

115g caster sugar

1 tsp vanilla extract

45g self-raising flour

30g cocoa powder

Caster sugar, for dusting

YOU WILL NEED

Piping bag with a 1cm tip

FOR THE MERINGUE MUSHROOMS

Line a baking tray with reusable silicone sheets or baking parchment. In a clean bowl, using an electric whisk, beat the egg whites for 3 to 4 minutes until they form stiff peaks.

Add the sugar, 1 tablespoon at a time, whisking continuously between additions. Rub a little meringue between your fingers to test and make sure no grains of sugar remain and, once smooth, whisk in the cream of tartar. Spoon the mixture into a piping bag with a 1cm tip, or cut 1cm off the bottom of your piping bag, if necessary.

Pipe seven to ten rounds, in varying sizes, and an equal number of 'stalks'. Use a wet finger to gently flatten any peaks, then bake in the oven for 1 hour. The meringues are ready when they peel off the paper easily. Leave to cool completely for 1 hour.

Once the meringues are cool, melt the chocolate in the microwave in a small bowl – check and stir every 10 to 15 seconds to ensure the chocolate does not split or start to cook. Once melted, carefully dip each meringue stalk into the chocolate before sticking it to the base of the mushroom caps. Dust the tops with a little cocoa powder. Leave in a cool place until you are ready to assemble your cake.

FOR THE CREAM FILLING

Whisk together the double cream and icing sugar until you have stiff peaks, then refrigerate until later. Finely chop the dried cherries or cranberries and place in a cup with 1 tablespoon of cold water to rehydrate.

FOR THE CHOCOLATE GANACHE

Put the cream in a small pan and warm over a medium heat until it starts to gently bubble at the edges. Remove from the heat and add the dark chocolate. Mix together until the chocolate has melted and is fully combined, then pour into a bowl and set aside for later.

FOR THE CHOCOLATE SPONGE

Grease a 30x20cm baking tin with butter and line with reusable silicone sheets or baking parchment. Add the eggs, sugar and vanilla extract to a large mixing bowl and whisk with an electric mixer until very pale and thick. It is ready when you can lift the whisk and make ribbon patterns on the surface of the mix. This can take a while, so be patient!

Sift in the flour and cocoa powder and carefully fold it through, using a spatula in a figure eight motion. Pour into the lined tin and smooth out until even. Bake for 10 to 12 minutes until just firm to the touch then remove from the oven.

Place a sheet of baking parchment onto a work surface and dust with caster sugar. Turn the warm sponge out onto the sugared paper and peel off the silicone sheet or baking parchment from its base. The caster sugar will help prevent the sponge sticking. Using a dinner knife, make an indentation in the sponge 15mm from one of the shorter edges. Gently roll up the sponge, and the paper along with it, starting at the indent. Leave the rolled up sponge to cool completely, leaving the paper underneath.

Once completely cool, it is ready to fill. Gently unroll the sponge and carefully spread with the whipped cream filling. Scatter over the chopped cherries or cranberries then re-roll the sponge, using the paper to help you. Cut a quarter of the cake from the end at a 45° angle. Transfer the larger piece of cake to a serving plate and position the cut portion in the middle to form a branch.

Whip up the chocolate ganache for 1 minute until soft and fluffy, then use a palette knife to spread the ganache over the cake. Use a fork to create a bark-like texture along the length of the cake, then arrange the mushrooms on the cake. Finish with a light dusting of icing sugar and enjoy!

LEMON AND GINGER CAKE

This cake looks very festive when decorated with biscuit trees and makes a nice alternative to a traditional Christmas cake. It's perfect when served after a frosty winter walk.

Serves: 6-8
Prep time: 45 minutes, plus 30 minutes chilling
Cooking time: 55 minutes
Oven temp: Cake: 180°C fan;
Biscuits: 160°C fan

FOR THE GINGER CAKE

150g self-raising flour

150g light soft brown sugar

1 tsp ground ginger

1 tsp mixed spice

¼ tsp bicarbonate of soda

60g salted butter

1 egg

1 tbsp golden syrup

100ml hot water

FOR THE BISCUITS

20g salted butter, softened

25g caster sugar

¼ tsp vanilla extract

½ tbsp milk

50g plain flour

½ tbsp icing sugar, for dusting

FOR THE LEMON ICING

15g salted butter, softened

75g icing sugar

1 tbsp lemon juice

YOU WILL NEED

Cookie cutters or a template

FOR THE GINGER CAKE

Grease and flour a round, 7-inch cake tin. In a bowl, combine the flour, brown sugar, spices and bicarbonate of soda. Using your fingers, rub the butter into the mixture until it resembles breadcrumbs. Add the egg, golden syrup and hot water and mix well with a wooden spoon until combined.

Pour the mixture into the prepared tin and bake in the middle of the oven for 30 to 45 minutes, or until golden brown and a cocktail stick inserted into the centre comes out clean. Leave to cool in the tin.

FOR THE BISCUITS

In a bowl, beat together the butter and sugar until creamy, then add the vanilla extract and milk and stir until combined. Add the flour and mix until it forms a dough. Wrap the dough in reusable food wrap and refrigerate for 30 minutes.

Transfer the biscuit dough to a lightly floured surface and roll out to approximately 5mm thick. Cut out three trees or other shapes of your choice. Transfer the biscuits to a tray lined with a reusable silicone sheet or baking parchment.

Bake for 10 to 12 minutes at 160°C, or until the edges are golden brown, then transfer to a wire rack and leave to cool. Once chilled, dust the biscuits with icing sugar.

FOR THE ICING

Beat the softened butter until creamy, then add the icing sugar and lemon juice and mix until smooth and combined. Using a spatula, frost the cake, adding small peaks to look like snow. To finish, arrange the biscuits on top of the cake. Finish with some sprigs of rosemary to decorate, if you like.

BAKER'S TIP

This cake works at any time of year; try cutting different biscuit shapes for different seasons.

Scan for template

SPICED FESTIVE JAMMY DODGER

A Christmassy take on a childhood favourite, these jammy dodgers are fun and delicious for all the family!

Makes: 15
Prep time: 45 minutes, plus 1 hour chilling
Cooking time: 10-12 minutes
Oven temp: 180°C fan

FOR THE BISCUITS

250g butter, at room temperature

200g sugar

1 egg

500g plain flour

1 tsp ground cinnamon

½ tsp ground nutmeg

½ tsp allspice

FOR THE SPICED JAM
(SEE BAKER'S TIP)

350g berry jam (or use your favourite jam)

½ cinnamon stick

¼ tsp allspice

5 cloves

YOU WILL NEED

Cookie cutters or a template

FOR THE BISCUITS

Cream the butter and sugar together, then add the egg and mix until well combined. Add the flour, cinnamon, nutmeg and allspice and mix slowly until a soft dough forms. Knead gently on a floured surface to form a round ball. Place in a bag or wrap in reusable food wrap and refrigerate for an hour.

Sprinkle flour over a work surface and split the dough into two balls. Roll one ball out thinly, about 3mm thick. Cut out circles and place on a baking tray lined with baking parchment. Repeat with the second ball, then gather the scraps and knead to form a ball again. Continue rolling out and cutting circles until all the dough has been used and there's an even number of biscuits.

Now, using small Christmas-themed cookie cutters or a sharp knife, cut out shapes from the middle of half of the biscuits whilst on the baking tray. This will stop the shapes distorting during transfer from the counter to the baking tray. Bake for 10 to 12 minutes, or until lightly golden – don't overcook them; they should be a very light brown colour. Place on a wire rack to cool.

FOR THE SPICED JAM

Add the jam to a small saucepan with the cinnamon stick, allspice, and cloves. Bring the jam to a gentle boil over a low heat, stirring all the time. Simmer for a couple of minutes then take the pan off the heat and allow to cool. Once cooled, remove the cinnamon stick and cloves.

Place a teaspoon of jam on each biscuit circle then place a biscuit with a shape cut out of it on top. Move as needed so the jam fills the cut-out shape, then dust with icing sugar. Allow the jam to set, then keep the biscuits in an airtight tin. They will last about a week (if you can resist them!).

BAKER'S TIP

If you're feeling lazy, you can skip the jam step and just use your favourite jam as it is. The biscuits will still be yummy, but not quite so Christmassy!

Scan for template

HOW TO USE UP LEFTOVERS

Waste not, want not! If you have leftovers, try the recipes and tips below. Most cakes and biscuits will also freeze well.

STALE BREAD
Edward's Chocolate French Toast (page 90)
Breadcrumb Plum Cake (page 74)
Chocolate Stale Bread Cake (page 78)

TOO MUCH OR SOUR MILK
Mum's Scones (page 30)
Jessica's Pancakes (page 26)
Custard, as in Rhubarb and Custard Doughnuts (page 38)
Use as a glaze for pastry and bread

A GLUT OF FRUIT, OR FRUIT ON THE TURN/PAST ITS BEST
Laura's Fruit Shortbread (page 106)
Dan's Fruit Crumble (page 44)
Baked Fruit Cheesecake (page 104)
Summer Fruit Drizzle (page 108)
Mum's Raspberry Jam, which can also be made using blackberries or blueberries (page 110)
Berry and Almond Cake (page 124)
Use old, brown bananas in Banana Chocolate Loaf (page 138)
Use the scraps from apples (you can freeze and save until you have enough) to make Apple Scrap Jelly (page 158)

A GLUT OF OR LEFTOVER VEGETABLES
Use the flesh of your Halloween pumpkins in Pumpkin Spice Cake (page 148)
Get your kids to eat vegetables with a Beetroot Brownie (page 136)
Use up leftover courgettes in a Courgette Cake (page 80)

EGG WHITES
Perfect for meringues, as in Lucy's Pavlova (page 82), Forest Floor Cupcakes (page 152), and Black Forest Yule (page 200)
Use in marzipan, as in Almond and Chocolate Croissants (page 34) and Dad's Stollen (page 194)
Perfect for royal icing, as in Lemon Daisy Biscuits (page 102), Cardamom and Orange Snowflake Biscuits (page 190), and Gingerbread House (page 184)
Use as a glaze for pastry and bread

EGG YOLKS
Use in custard or marzipan, as in Rhubarb and Custard Doughnuts (page 38), Almond and Chocolate Croissants (page 34), Deanne's Strawberry Choux au Craquelin (page 76), and Cherry and Almond Viennese Whirls (page 100)
Raspberry and White Chocolate Eclairs (page 28)
Use in a lemon or orange curd, as in Spiced Easter Egg Biscuits (page 56)
Chocolate and Hazelnut Babka Knots (page 140)
Use as a glaze for pastry and bread

STALE OR TOO MUCH CAKE
Use in trifles, summer puddings, and Tiffin (page 40)

STALE OR TOO MANY BISCUITS
Biscuits will re-crisp in a low oven; simply lay them out on a baking sheet and put in a low oven, about 50°C, until crisp once more
Once crisp, use in Baked Fruit Cheesecake (page 104), Refrigerator Cake (page 150) or Tiffin (page 40)

ACKNOWLEDGEMENTS

Firstly, I must thank Kayley Miles, who joined Honeywell Bakes in 2018 and has baked, photographed and taste tested about half of the recipes in this book. Kayley's baking skills, flavour combinations, and dedication have been the main reason our baking kit and subscription sides of the business have been a success. Who knows where we'd be without her! Deanne Young has worked alongside Kayley for a fair amount of this journey, and her creativity has helped no end.

A MASSIVE, MASSIVE thank you to Laura Slack, my sister and sidekick since I was two years old, who joined Honeywell Bakes in 2021 to help us with sustainability and gaining our B Corp certification. She has spent many, many hours baking and writing, discussing, and helping with this book. Without her, it wouldn't exist.

Thank you to my husband Colin, who bought me my trusty KitchenAid stand mixer many years ago when Honeywell Bakes first started and put up with biscuits being iced all over the house for several years before we moved to a dedicated premises.

My family is big and chaotic and a little bit crazy, but they all contribute to everything: Helen Honeywell, my mum, who is my inspiration for everything; Paul Honeywell, my amazing dad, whose creativity is wonderful; and my siblings Laura, Daniel, Rosie, Lucy, Dominic, and Rhiannon, as well as their partners Andrew, Emily, Robbie, Sim and Andy.

Thank you to my children, Isabella, Jessica and Edward, who have given honest (sometimes too honest!) feedback on the bakes, and who have all baked since they could stand on a stool at the kitchen worktop. Also to "The Cousins", Louis, Jonah, Rosanna and Leo, who are always wanting treats.

And to our wonderful, all-women team at Honeywell Bakes: Kayley Miles, Alex Rigby, Jane Garner, Lucy Prigmore, Gemma Goode, Holly Barrett, Stacey Dorgun, Deanne Young, Angela Mayers, Tegan Cooke, Clare Horn, Cheryl Lafratta, Abby Snell, Polly Nisbett, Alice Watkins, Charlotte Basson, Alice Colyer, Hollie Davies and Laura Slack. Thank you all – you have tasted everything willingly (never say no to cake!) and offered feedback and advice.

Thank you to John and Guy for always being so helpful and allowing our business to thrive.

And thank you to Meze Publishing, who have helped us through the process of writing our first book.

BUSINESSES AND RESOURCES WE LOVE

INGREDIENTS

Crowdfarming (crowdfarming.com) – boxes of fruit or nuts

LittlePod Vanilla (littlepod.co.uk)

Wildfarmed Flour (wildfarmed.com)

Doves Farm (dovesfarm.co.uk) – organic flour

Matthews Cotswold (cotswoldflour.com)

Pipers Farm (pipersfarm.com) – regeneratively farmed eggs and butter

Riverford (riverford.co.uk) – fruit, veg and other daily essentials

Abel and Cole (abelandcole.co.uk) – organic eggs, butter, and weekly deliveries of planet friendly essentials

Whole Foods (buywholefoodsonline.co.uk) – dried fruit and nuts

Shipton Mill (shipton-mill.com)

Suma (suma-store.coop) – organic sugar

EQUIPMENT

If You Care (ifyoucare.co.uk) – baking parchment, cupcake cases, and other natural household and kitchen items, available across the UK, both in-store and online

Falcon Enamelware (falconenamelware.com) – good quality enamel bakeware

KitchenAid (kitchenaid.co.uk)

Nordic Ware – bundt tins, based in America but available in a variety of UK stores

PME (pmecake.com) - piping tips

CLEANING

Seep (theseepcompany.com)

Fill (fillrefill.co)

Method (methodproducts.co.uk)

Smol (smol.com)

OceanSaver (ocean-saver.com)

WEBSITES

Wicked Leeks (wickedleeks.riverford.co.uk)

Soil Association (soilassociation.org)

WRAP (wrap.ngo)

Pesticide Action Network (pan-uk.org)

B Corp Directory (bcorporation.net/en-us/find-a-b-corp)

Royal Society (royalsociety.org)

Friends of the Earth (friendsoftheearth.uk)

Six Inches of Soil (sixinchesofsoil.org)

PAN UK (pan-uk.org/dirty-dozen)

BOOKS

World of Books (worldofbooks.com) - for second hand books

Eating to Extinction, by Dan Salidino

One Pot, Pan, Planet, by Anna Jones

Compost Kate, by Kate Flood

Wilding, by Isabella Tree

River Cottage Handbook: Preserves, by Pam Corbin

How Bad Are Bananas?, by Mike Berners-Lee

GROWING FRUIT AND VEG

Pot Gang (potgang.co.uk)

Heritage Organic Seeds (heritiageorganicseeds.com)

Real Seeds (realseeds.co.uk)

Charles Dowding (charlesdowding.co.uk)

FOOD WASTE

Olio (olioapp.com)

Share Waste (sharewaste.com)

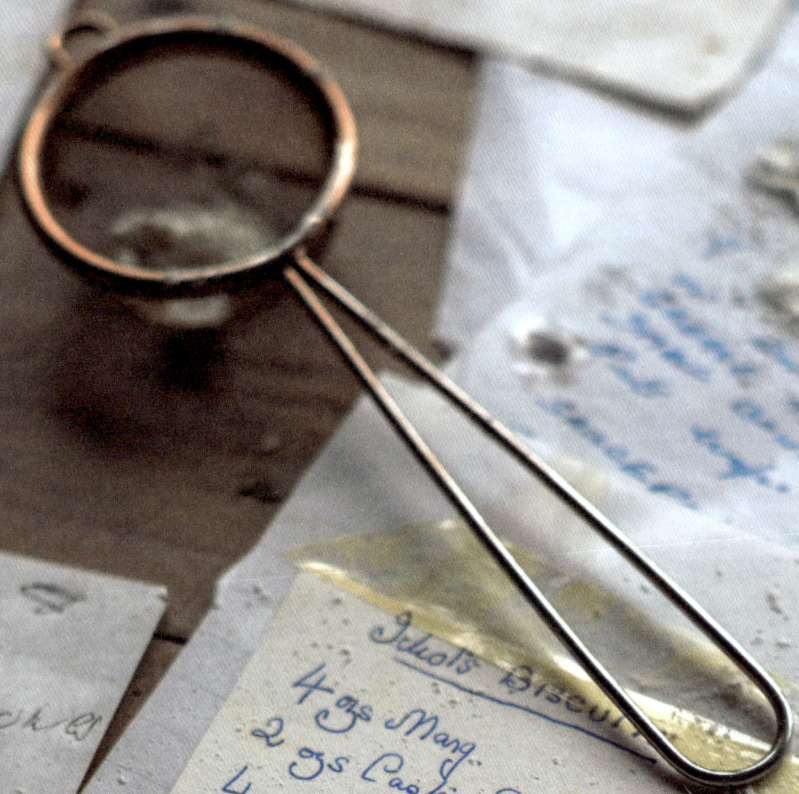

Idiots Biscuits

4 ozs Marg.
2 ozs Castor Sugar.
4 ozs Plain Flour.
One Tablesps. of Cocoa.
½ Tablesp of Vanilla Essence.

Method

Cream Marg and Sugar
well, add rest of ingredients in a
well. Roll into little balls, place
on greased baking tray. Press each
with back of a fork dipped in hot
water. Bake for 20 mins (25 mins)
180°C Gas Mark 4. Leave to cool,
fill with cooled ... before putting away